CREATIVE EVENTS

CREATIVE EVENTS
Edition 2010

Author: Jacobo Krauel

Graphic design & production: Cuboctaedro

Collaborator: Oriol Vallés, graphic designer & Roberto Bottura, architect

Text: Contributed by the architects, edited by Jay Noden

© Carles Broto i Comerma

Jonqueres, 10, 1-5

08003 Barcelona, Spain

Tel.: +34-93-301-21-99

Fax: +34-93-301-00-21

info@linksbooks.net

www.linksbooks.net

CREATIVE EVENTS

LINKS

INTRODUCTION

Exciting corporate events...planned by architects and designers!

Creative Events explores new opportunities for design professionals. Dozens of projects, complete with commentary, full-color photos, and plans.

Renowned architects, artists and designers convey their ideas by way of new techniques and approaches and previously unexplored materials. Their strength lies in the imagination of their designers, which blurs the borders of what can and can't be done. These projects demonstrate how ephemeral architecture can reach out and surprise us. They draw attention to the role creativity plays in events and introduce elements that may become a source of inspiration for professionals of the future.

scape-visionscape

Hannover, Germany

The debate on creating a landmark building for EXPO 2000 which, like the Eiffel Tower or the Atomium, would then endure after the exposition had come and gone, spawned the idea behind the virtual architecture of 'visionscape'. Given the highly topical architectural discourse at the turn of the century on computer-generated, immaterial spaces, the design team at 3deluxe felt it only logical that the world exposition should be represented by a virtual symbol. The bud-like shape of 'visionscape' thrust upwards through Hall 25 to a height of 2 km (1.2 miles) above the trade-fair complex. Within the hall itself, this vision was then implemented as a physically tangible section of the immaterial architecture: in the form of 'scape', an interactive landscape of events.

The "Young People's Media Worlds" were part of the program of cultural events at the World Exposition, where they took up 4000 sqm (43 000 sqft) of hall space. The intention was to encourage an experimental approach and a creative and conscious attitude towards New Media. The architectural design was developed from the conceptual approach of genetic architecture, which achieved its first realization within the inner 'scape' world. Softly shaped structures materialized the fluid framework of virtual space. 'Scape' was designed as a multi-layered perception area, enabling simultaneous experiences of the physical and the virtual. The visitors could alter the surrounding atmosphere by means of interactive installations. These interfaces linked the real space of 'scape' with the virtual communication area of 'visionscape', which released the project from all dependence on time and space, transferring it to a level with global access. The non-material architecture of 'visionscape' symbolizes the intensification of global, location independent communication. It abrogates the temporary and local restrictions of 'scape' by transferring it into the endless virtual sphere of the Internet. This differentiated overlay of information and space was explained in an animated film, demonstrating the creation of 'visionscape'.

Design: 3deluxe
Client: EXPO 2000
Photographs: 3deluxe

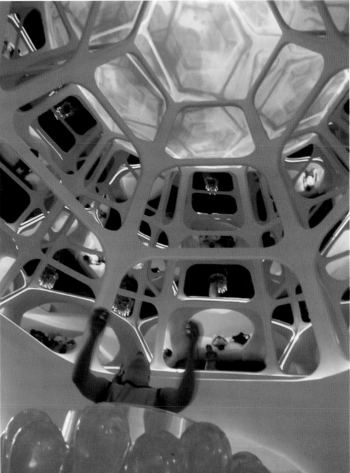

A number of Club Evenings took place in the memory lounge. This series of events ended with an outstanding performance on the final day of the World Exhibition. A sequence of three DJ sets in Germany, Japan and the USA was transmitted live into the Internet as a video and audio stream. The virtual level of the 'scape' project linked these venues together to form a trans-continental communication area. The general public in front of the Expo Hall were able to view the entire session on the 25 m (82 ft) high water screens of the Flambée Show. Their liquid matrix, partially sprayed by the wind, symbolized the virtual and fleeting nature of this media event. Digital traces of the temporary staging could be found after the event on the 'visionscape' website.

Tiffany & Company Gehry Jewelry Launch

Los Angeles, California, USA

Tiffany & Company hired Los Angeles architecture, industrial design and fabrication firm Ball-Nogues to create the environment for Frank Gehry's gala party celebrating the launch of Gehry's signature jewelry designs. Held on a closed portion of Rodeo Drive in Beverly Hills, California the production featured temporary constructions that filled the street, created spectacle, and honored the materiality of Gehry's early work. Designers Benjamin Ball and Gaston Nogues developed a new manufacturing process using corrugated cardboard to create voluptuous curved walls, furniture, and bars for the event. They found inspiration in the process and material Gehry employed in his legendary "Easy Edges" furniture of the 1970's.

Ball-Nogues designed and oversaw the construction of walls and furniture that required laminating over 25 000 strips of curved, industrially cut cardboard. A wall structure, half a block long and curved like the human body, was constructed from 4000 strips of cardboard sandwiched together. "Peep show" display windows, inspired by Marcel Duchamp's *Étant donnés*, punctuated the wall. Tightly framed views of live nude models, wearing nothing but the Gehry jewelry, served as living "body as landscape" advertisements. Twenty-four ottomans, no two alike and distributed across the event space, invited 600 guests to explore alternative ways of sitting.

The lamination method developed for the project represents another direction in the material and process derived explorations of Ball-Nogues. Incredibly strong and capable of supporting the weight of several people, the laminates operate like shells (integrating structure and skin) rather than surfaces - which need the support of a skeletal armature. The pieces reorient the viewer's notions of standard corrugated cardboard from a raw packaging material to a substance with structural potential at an architectural scale and capable of being used to fashion sensuous compound curving forms that resemble wood sculpted with a computer controlled (CNC) router.

Design: Benjamin Ball and Gaston Nogues
Photographs: contributed by Ball-Nogues Studio
Project Team: Sam Gehry, Jonathan Ward
Fabricator: Ethos Design
Client: Tiffany & Company

15

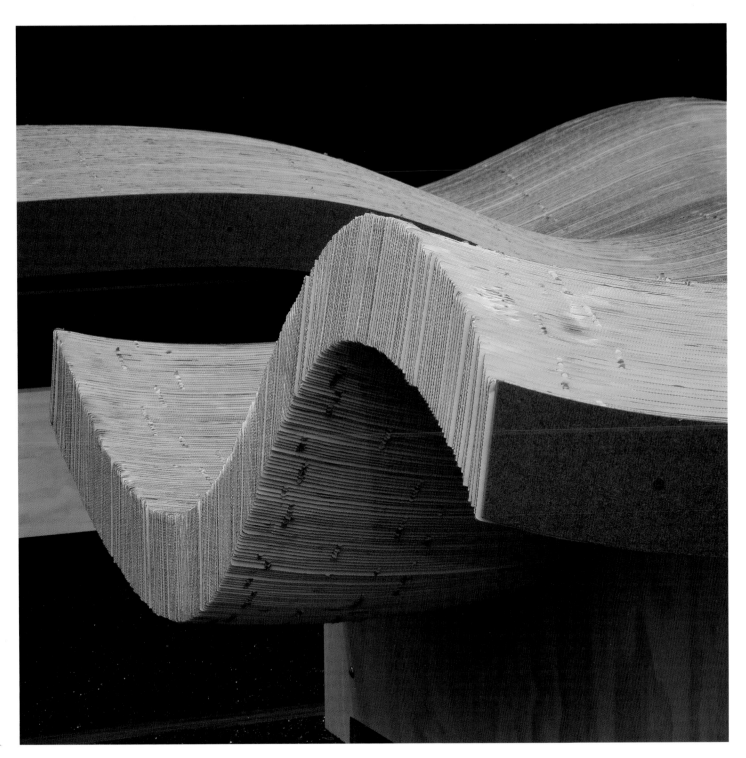

1. Screen - LED or projection
2. DJ area
3. Second level platform for DJ only
4. Scaffolding
5. Duvatine
6. Box with curtain, 45 cm (18 inches)
7. Platform for models

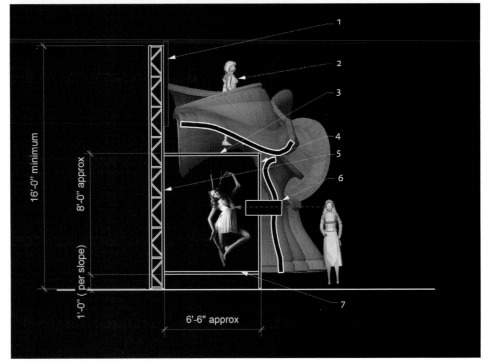

Cityscape

Brussels, Belgium

This impressive wooden sculpture was created by Belgium artist Arne Quinze to be in situ for one year in the Quartier Louise district in Brussels. "Cityscape" was sponsored by the car brand Mini. The connection between the car and the project is, according to Quinze, that *"Mini has managed to change the face of the city. It's a vehicle that prompts reactions, since it's almost impossible not to notice. Mini, to me, is a good example of successful communication."* The idea was for Cityscape to open to the public at the same time as the world premier of the new Mini clubman car.

The colossal installation is 18 m (60 ft) high and was built on 12 meter-high (40 ft) wooden stilts. Carrying the same ambiguous traits as her earlier siblings, of which Uchronia (a giant wooden sculpture, last year built in Nevada desert) is the most striking example, Cityscape attracts Brussels inhabitants to this suburb like a magnet. It encourages interaction and injects new energy into a somewhat uncared for neighborhood. Floating in the air, it provides shelter for curious visitors, as well as a place for contemplation and silence. The tranquil environment it creates is enhanced on sunny days as the sunlight filters through the wooden beams generating an ever-changing play of light and shadow on the ground below.

The eye-catching sculpture looks as if it has been made from thousands of giant matchsticks and is intended to represent frozen movement. It seems, when seen from a distance, as if pure movement is keeping this volatile structure in the air. Due to its immense size, 40 m (130 ft)long and 25 m (80 ft) wide, Cityscape is impossible to ignore and absorbs the attention of anyone passing by, thus transforming into a powerful tool for communication.

As well as being a medium for bringing a community together and revitalizing an urban area, Cityscape is also an ecologically sound project, since all the wood used will be fully regenerated and recycled when the time comes for its disassembly.

Design: Arne Quinze
Client: Mini
Photographs: contributed by Quinze&Milan

MTV Awards Brazil

São Paulo, Brazil

This surprising and colorful installation was designed and produced for Brazil's 2006 MTV awards, which took place in Sao Paulo, Brazil. Sao Paulo-based architectural studio Nelson Fiedler was responsible for the event architecture. The company specializes in membrane architecture and tensile structures and is known for their creative and daring projects.

The creative drive for this project was born from the idea that the awards were to reveal who is the year's best musician, or in other words the year's music 'genius'. This led the design team to consider how best to represent the search for the 'genie' of music. As a result they designed tents that resembled the genie's bottle with a center that protrudes imitating the long neck of the fairy tale version of the vessel. As well as being bottle-shaped the tents were designed to have a strong Arabic appearance lending further emphasis to the design concept. The decoration inside the tents followed from their exteriors, but with each displaying its own unique interior design.

The structure was made from 3D metal trusses and then covered with a customized synthetic PVC canvas. No pigment was used for the canvas thereby allowing the structures to change color as the lights inside changed. Furthermore, being translucent meant the tents were able to receive back projection. Aside from the impressive visual effect, the tents also made the most of their space, with generously spacious interiors, which were free of columns or other obstacles.

Design: Nelson Fiedler
Client: MTV Brazil
Photographs: contributed by Nelson Fiedler

Evoke

York, UK

A specially commissioned project for Illuminating York 2007 in northern England, Evoke is a massive animated projection that lights up the façade of York Minster in response to the public, who use their own voices to "evoke" colorful light patterns that emerge at the building's foundations and soar up towards the sky, giving the surface a magical feeling as it melts with color.

The cathedral, built to conceptually link earth to the heavens, has been a site for the conveyance of words, dreams and aspirations for hundreds of years. The façade is designed to orient the gazes of passers-by upwards. As an attempt to continue this tradition, the patterns of Evoke are generated in real-time by the words, sounds, music and noises produced collectively by the public, determined by their particular voice characteristics. The colors will skim the surface of the Minster, pour round its features and crevasses, emerging finally near the top of the façade where they will sparkle high overhead.

People with voices of different frequencies, rhythms or cadences will be able to evoke quite different magical patterns upon the surface of the building - a staccato chirping will result in a completely different set of visual effects to a long howl for example, blending old and new to continue animating the façade of the Minster.

Design: Haque Design + Research.
Original concept developed with Ai Hasegawa
Collaborators: Rory McCarthy, curator and project organiser, York Council; CW Scaffolding; and Nick Schneider, projection supervisor.
Projectors: Kindly supplied by XL Video.
Photographs: Haque Design + Research Ltd

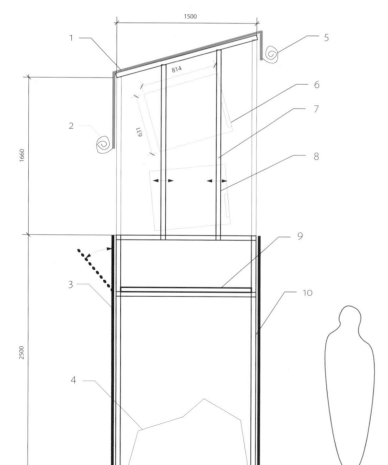

1. Tin roof
2. Tarpaulin (rolled up during use)
3. Cladding (plastic or plywood)
4. Sand ballast
5. Tarpaulin (use rope over roof to roll up during use)
6. Christies Roadster projector mounted to vertical poles
7. Cantilevered bar for suspended microphones
8. Adjustable vertical scaffolding poles for mounting projectors
9. Plywood platform for distro units and computers
10. Scaffolding with bracing as req'd

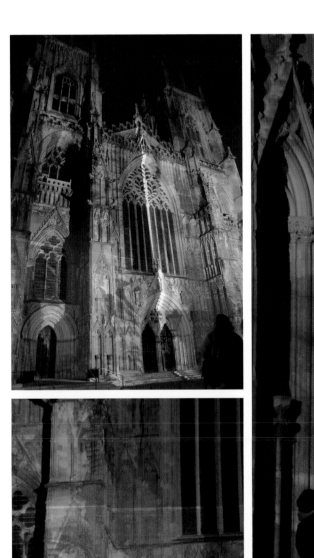

kubik

Barcelona, Spain

kubik was a radically innovative nightclub, developed by Balestra Berlin, which brought together architecture, light and music. It was located in the Forum venue in Barcelona, at the time a relatively new place in the city, which had still not been fully embraced by the local population. The setting was ideal: open to the sky and beside the sea.

This unique project had been launched for the first time in Berlin the previous summer and, in a similar vein, revitalized an unused site of the city. It was celebrated by the press for its unconventional fusion of design, light and club event as well as for successfully reanimating a fallow area within the city of Berlin. In Barcelona kubik was programmed for the limited time of four months during the summer, a time when the city is full of people looking for a party. Especially one by the beach.

279 illuminated industrial tanks piled one on top of each other, formed a spectacular design object of walls and columns. Inside kubik, visitors experienced illuminated cubes, whose light geometry was programmed to change constantly to the rhythm of music. The club was installed on two different areas of the Forum. An above ground level section of the site's photovoltaic pergola was the venue for a bar illuminated in magenta, while down at the dockside, the cubes that comprised kubik's club venue gleamed in a dazzling green.

DJs were invited from all over the world, especially from the renowned German scene, along with national musicians and local talents from Barcelona. The disc jockeys were joined by light jockeys, who interacted visually with the music, affording a more organic feel to the club venue.

With its originality, energy and charisma kubik set out to reclaim the Forum as a truly public space, and to make it a venue known and liked by locals and tourists alike.

Design: Balestra Berlin in cooperation with Modulorbeat and LightLife
Producer: Balestra Berlin
Photographs: contributed by Balestra Berlin

Coke Pavilion at Fat Music Festival

Chiangmai, Thailand

Thailand's Fat Festival is an annual music event where national bands, as well as groups from neighboring Asian countries are invited to take to the stage. Having become a successful event in Bangkok the festival organizers decided to move it to the northern province of Chiang Mai. As co-sponsors of the event, Coca-cola had a booth there, which promoted their product. Apostrophy's, a newly formed group of graphic designers based in Thailand, were commissioned by the multinational company to design a booth that would entice festival goers into the space to sample the refreshing drink.

Working in close collaboration with the client, Apostrophy's established a key phrase around which to base the design: "Coke Kao-Soy". The complete phrase is Thai for "Coke in the Lane", while "Kao-soy" is a local dish consisting of northern rice noodles with coconut milk soup. The team therefore decided to create a space that would bear some kind of similarity to a rice field as people entered, as if they were walking into a lane of rice.

Thick rubber tubes were suspended from the ceiling of the booth in such a way as to create a series of translucent curtains, thus establishing the "rice lanes". The tubes were clear but were intermingled around the perimeter with neon tube lights, which hung from the ceiling at different heights and produced a red tinted glow. When the neon lights shone through the tubes they became an array of diff erent shades of red and pink. Seen from a distance the booth displayed the combination of whites and reds that the Coca Cola brand has become known for.

Inside the booth, cylindrical containers were spread about like "Crop Circles", each one being a base for an activity, as well as providing free samples of the drink. One such activity was "Million Faces" where faces of celebrities hung from the ceiling and visitors could have their photos taken surrounded by famous people. There was also the "DIY" space where people could paint their own t-shirts and bags and the "Fog Shutter Wall" where the tubes represented a vertical paddy field and were filled with cold steam, which was then released refreshing those who walked through.

Design: Apostrophy's
Client: Coca-Cola
Event date: February 2008
Design Director: Pantavit Lawaroungchok
Producer: Sanchai Chotinoppakun
Art Director: Kosin Poonkasem
Photography: Sirichai Luengvisutsiri

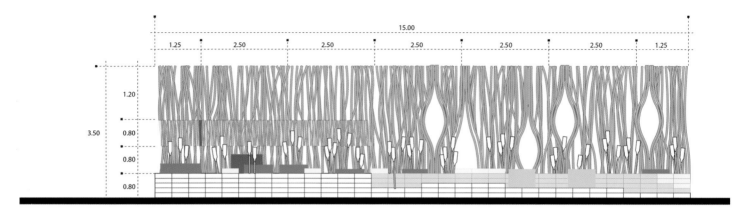

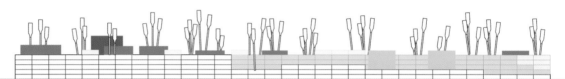

In "Million Faces" a multitude of celebrity heads were suspended from the ceiling at different heights offering visitors the chance to have their photos taken alongside the rich and famous.

Art Wheel

Frankfurt, Germany

Frankfurt's riverbank is a unique focal point for artistic diversity. The museums here contain world-class collections – and at the 2005 Museum Riverbank Festival, the Art Wheel brought them out into the public eye. The aim of this Big Wheel-cum-media installation was to create a large, memorable central symbol for the festival motto: "World Culture, Cultural World". It also set out to heighten public awareness of the diversity and international significance of the cultural treasures in the Rhine-Main region.

Art Wheel provided a surprising forum for Frankfurt's cultural landscape by uniting icons from two different worlds. Standing 40 m high (130 ft) and clad in 450 sqm (4800 sqft) of canvas, the installation became a new city landmark that revolved against the backdrop of the evening skyline. A never-ending stream of light, media animations and projections spoke of 100 masterpieces from sixteen museums. Art Wheel offered a gentle ride through the styles, colors and forms of different ages. The neutral architecture of the frame provided the stage, while the surrounding high-rise buildings formed the stage set.

A graphic globe transformed the Big Wheel into a world sphere – a symbol of the festival motto and an intelligent blend of yesteryear's fairground ride and today's media installations. Sensors matched the physical and digital movements by synching digital projections to the motions of the wheel.

Each gondola represented a different museum; when picked by the pointer, a corresponding animation ran on the wheel's hub while the guests inside learned more about "their" museum and the masterpieces it contained. With its fascinating blend of grandeur, beauty and momentum, Art Wheel was a thrilling symbol for the 2005 Riverbank Festival.

Client: Tourismus+Congress GmbH Frankfurt
Design: Atelier Markgraph
Spatial communication and design: Atelier Markgraph
Creative direction: Stefan Weil, Roland Lambrette
Media and graphic design: Kristin Trümper, Jan Schmelter
Project management: Andreas Behl
Ferris Wheel owner: Sascha Hanstein, Otfried Hanstein
Lighting technology: Procon Event Engineering GmbH, Christoph Hahnl, Eberhard Neer
Video technology: XL Video, Velten GmbH, Ulrich Velten
Lighting design: Dietrich Körner
Digital media system design: Meso, digital media systems, Sebastian Oschatz, and others.

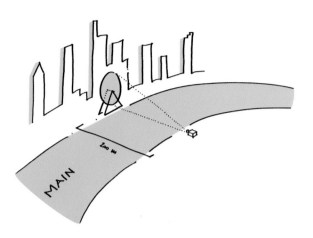

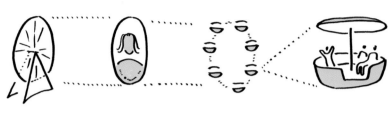

Cyberhelvetia.ch

Biel, Switzerland

3deluxe's projects seek to create a dualistic environment harmoniously blending artificial and natural, fictitious and real, familiar and unusual elements to form a "mixed reality." Virtuality is not defined as a substitute, but as an integrative supplement to reality as we experience it. Virtually constructed realities always reference the world of objects in a host of different ways, helping foster a new and holistic perception of a specific environment. This new sense of space is generated by multi-sensory stimuli, synaesthetic effects and atmospheres that appeal to the emotions. Exhibitions devised by 3deluxe call on visitors to playfully and individually explore their surroundings. The many layers to their exhibitions give birth to a variety of potential interpretations.

The lakeside baths at the Arteplage Biel-Bienne offered visitors the chance to experience the truly tangible world of "Cyberhelvetia.ch." Just like traditional Swiss swimming baths the exhibition pavilion was a place of personal encounters and communication. Nowadays, however communication can occur in many different ways regardless of location and language. Even a "joint swim together" no longer requires real water. Instead visitors were able to dive head first into the multi-layered atmosphere of a virtually expanded reality and bathe in light and sound. Inside the "Cyberhelvetia" pavilion tradition and the future, reality and virtuality, and nature and technology were amalgamated into a novel and fascinating experience of space. The glass pool in the middle of the exhibition replaced the real swimming pool. On the surface and along the sides of the luminous glass block various forms of play offered the opportunity to make contact with other guests in an unconventional way. The pool was filled with virtual water, which was enriched by the exhibition visitors both on the spot or on the Internet with imaginative life forms. The reciprocal interaction between real and virtually present people and artificial life forms constantly created new atmospheric images on the pool's surface almost giving the impression that a living organism was being created.

Idea, concept, supervision, planning: 3deluxe
General contractor and technical director: system modern GmbH
Media systems design, idea, animation: meso
Sound design: Hagü Schmitz
Web design 'vivarium' website: Screenbow
Software design 'Cy.Bee' game: meso
Sound design 'Cy.Bees': Ecki Ehlers
Glass pool: Dätwyler AG
Statics glass pool: Schlaich, Bergermann und Partner
Constructions: Gecco GmbH
Floor covering, seating elements: Kruse Systems
Tempur: Tempur Deutschland
Lighting, special effects: Karlen Lichttechnik
Lighting: Lightpower GmbH
Nylon matrix: Steelworks
Various glass elements: Glas Schröder
'Soundbeam' speakers: Sennheiser
Audio mixer: Teac Deutschland
Speakers: Ruag Electronics
Timing 'Soundbeam' speakers: i:cue
Communication technology 'infogirl': Riedel
Graphic design (exhibition): 3deluxe
Photographs: Emanuel Raab for 3deluxe

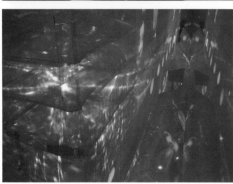

The Lift

London, UK

The project came about in response to the success of the London International Festival of Theatre (Lift). The Festival aimed to open theatre to Londoners and give everyone the opportunity to experience it. However as it became more popular performances began to take place in bigger venues and the festival was in danger of losing its original objective. The Lift was intended to go out in search of an audience who may otherwise not attend a theatre production. In keeping with the desire to involve the public, 200 East London residents and several arts organizations took part in a total of 30 workshops during 6 months to explore the space's potential uses.

The final theatre/circus tent was put together by Unusual Rigging, a company with a wealth of experience in demountable event architecture. The main structure is made from a standard steel-truss framework, which can be erected and taken apart with relative ease. Once disassembled it is stored inside two shipping containers, which also act as the project's box office. A tensile fabric roof covers the structure opening out as it reaches down to the ground. The building's unusual shape is a result of combining an oval floor plan with a rectangular roof. The whole structure sits on a large platform and is accessed via stairs and a ramp. The building's height allows the Lift to relate to the façades of nearby buildings and to be seen as a recognizable landmark.

The pattern that decorates the outside of the building, and ensures it won't be missed, was based on a standard quilt pattern. This was distributed to everyone involved in the project who then colored it in. The resulting images were then merged together to from the colorful exterior.

In order to deal with the multi-purpose nature of the project the architects designed a series of mobile elements. Three acoustically insulated silver domes equipped with programmable lighting hang from the ceiling. Curtains can be attached to each of these offering the possibility of creating three new rooms.

The main elevation is dominated by a billboard that can be moved up and down. When lowered it reveals a space at the top where the building's steel structure can be seen, providing ventilation and allowing light to enter. When raised the interior is blacked out. The sign can also be replaced by a screen that uses back projection or taken out entirely.

Design: AOC
Client: London International Festival of Theatre
Structural engineer: Momentum
Theatre consultant: Charcoal Blue
Acoustic consultant: Vanguardia Consulting
Environmental engineer: XCO2
Contractor: Unusual Rigging
Subcontractors:
Steelwork: Sheetfabs
Fabric: Architen LandrellFabric Printing: Media Co
Deployables Inflate: Curtains and voiles Acre
JeanCurtain track: Triple E
Photographs: contributed by AOC

2008 Realised and erected in:
• Stratford Park, East London
• Festival Square,
Southbank Centre, London
• Shoreditch Park, North London
2009 touring Thames Gateway

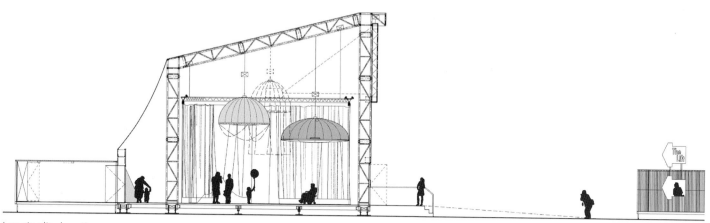

Longitudinal section

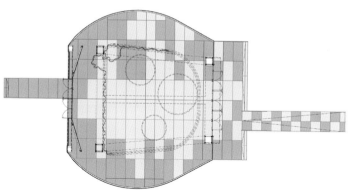

Plan

Cutting patterns for The Lift

1: Take a quilting tile, the 'Best of All'
2: Add fill, colour and pattern of your choice within the density constraints
3: Patch a quilt together

6: Overlay a distinct pattern
5: Distort the pattern to fit the fabrication strips
6: Number the strips

7: The Lift Elevations
8: Apply the Quilt
9: Number the strips
9: Translate the pattern
10: Fabricate the membrane

① ② ③ ④ ⑤ ⑥ ⑦ ⑧ ⑨ ⑩

< 30 %

> 70 %

Pattern development

The Sound of Squares

Germany, various cities

In the summer of 2007, the German city of Mannheim celebrated its 400th anniversary. To mark the occasion, the City of Squares, known as such thanks to the grid layout of its urban plan, decided it wanted to enhance its familiarity and popularity nationwide by way of an activity that tied in with the long-term positioning strategy called Mannheim 2 "Living in Squares." The idea was to give people an emotional and appealing taste of the city (and whet their appetite for more) by attracting strong media attention and generating large numbers of personal contacts. The architecture also needed to be travel-proof, as the project was to cover four locations and 3 500 kilometers in 53 days.

To mark the anniversary, the city sent a multimedia cube on a tour of Germany. On board was a vast array of audio files, in keeping with Mannheim's reputation for music. The basic shape of the project was inspired by the famous squares on the Mannheim city map.

The Sound of Squares was separated into three zones. The first, Seating Cubes, consisted of large red cubes. When visitors sat down on one of these cubes they triggered off audio files. This collaborative form of audio interaction modified the "pulse of the city" which was transmitted by the cube. The second zone, dubbed the Audio Forest, was an audio blog from Mannheim for the residents of the tour's host cities.

The third zone was the Interactive Audio Laboratory, where anyone who visited had the opportunity of creating their own music mix. Small, convenient sample cubes acted as containers for audio building blocks. All visitors needed to do was dock on to listen to an array of beats, bass riffs and vocals, which they could choose from to create their tune. Alternatively they could record their own samples. The final "Mannheim Mixdown" was then put together at the mixing console and the audio track could be saved onto a record cube so that the visitor could take it home with them.

Client: Stadtmarketing Mannheim GmbH, Mannheim
Idea, Concept and Production: Atelier Markgraph GmbH (AM)
Creative Direction: Stefan Weil (AM)
Art Direction: Jan Schmelter (AM), Kristin Trümper (AM)
Team: Christopher Alker, Lars Uwe Bleher, Christina Cziepluch, Markus Dittrich, Rui Filipe, Alexander Hanowski, Stefanie Heinrich, Johanno Hess, Tobias Kehrberger, Christina Loeffler-Kitzinger, Angela Kratz, Andrea Moseler, Uwe Müller, Jürgen Schultz-Anker, Klaus-Peter Texter, André Urban (all:AM)
Software development and Sound Lab programming: meso | digital media systems design (Team: Sebastin Oschatz, Ingolf Heinsch, David Dessens et al.)
Composition 'Pulse of the City' and artistic audio consultant for Sound Lab: Chriz Oz
Exhibit construction: Freisteel, Reichelsheim
Media technology: Procon Frankfurt
Client: Stadtmarketing Mannheim
Photographs: Thomas Tröster, Ralph Larmann

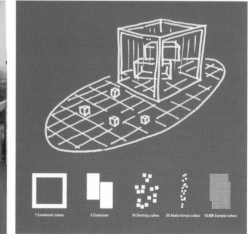

| 1 Landmark cubes | 2 Container | 16 Seating cubes | 20 Audio forest cubes | 10.000 Sample cubes |

"There's not a problem that I can't fix – 'cause I can do it in the mix"

Closing Ceremony 2006 World Cup

Berlin, Germany

On the occasion of the Closing Ceremony of the 2006 World Cup which took place on the 9th of July before the final game in the Berlin Olympic Stadium 3deluxe's progressive design language and their scenographic ideas contributed to the sympathetic contemporary image of Germany that was presented to the world audience. Commissioned by André Heller, the interdisciplinary group developed the scenographic design including all stage buildings as well as the costume and sound design for the ten-minute show.

More than 200 performers and FIFA show acts Il Divo and Shakira were included in the lively staging on the staircase of the Marathon Gate. Fan drummers and dancers, flag bearers as colorful ambassadors of the FIFA continental zones and street dancers from Berlin offered a euphoric performance on and around the stage. More than sixty performers created a moving, graphically designed backdrop by waving textile umbrellas as screens over their heads following a sophisticated choreography. The printed motive referred in its abstract form to the most important stage of the World Cup – in a green and white composition of pitch and lines.

The stage located halfway up the ranks contrasted effectively with the monolithic architecture of the Marathon Gate by means of its dynamic shape. The winners' podium took up the dynamic lines of the stage and was thus clearly distanced from the usually conventionally designed platforms. The socket positioned beside the pitch on which the trophy was visibly displayed during the final match was also part of 3deluxe's integral design concept.

Design: 3deluxe
Concept, planning, art direction: 3deluxe
Architecture, stage buildings consultancy:
Gecco Scene Construction GmbH
Audio technology consultancy:
Werner Audio GmbH & Co. KG
Lighting technology consultancy: Showtec GmbH
interior Project development and management,
realisation: system modern GmbH
Choreography: Doug Jack
Sound design: Frank Zerban
Client: OC FIFA 2006 World Cup
Photographs: Emanuel Raab for 3deluxe

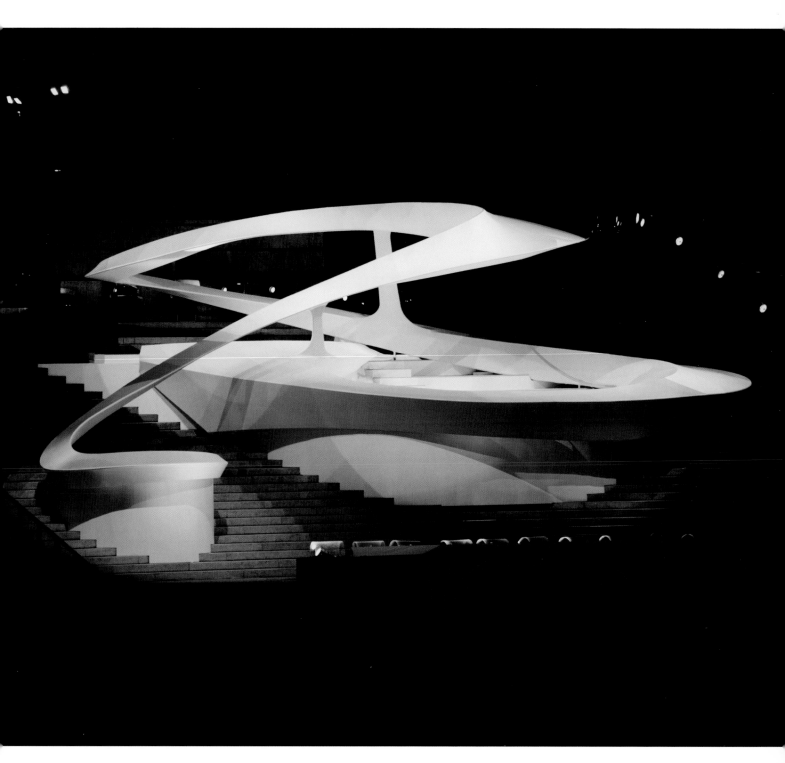

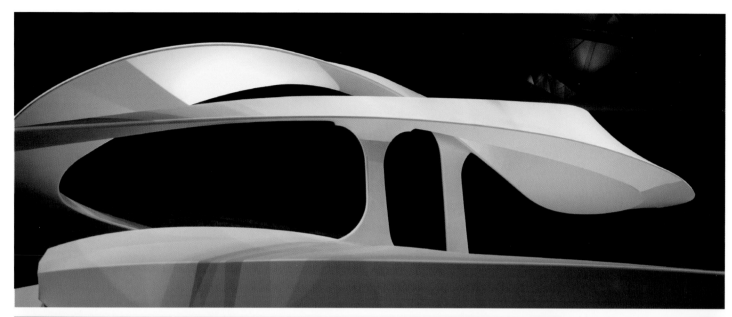

Tiger Translate Finale

Bangkok, Thailand

The second annual Tiger Translate Music and Art Festival, sponsored by Tiger Beer, brought together a colorful array of musical acts and artistic production, including street art and illustrations by famous artists. The event took place inside the Danneramit Park, one of Bangkok's major outdoor venues. Momentum, the festival organizers, commissioned local, emerging design studio Apostrophy's to design the space, dividing the area into different art zones and providing exciting construction details.

The brief for the project centered about the words "winning" and "translation", the former being a reference to the competitions that are held at the festival for artists, and the latter referring to the name of the festival itself. The designers, working from this premise, developed an idea based on related words such as winning, passion, success etc. The design was also meant to allude to the site's previous function as a fun park.

The main area designed by Apostrophy's was the Typopark. This was a space filled with large panels cut into words, such as those mentioned above, and arranged to form a maze of ideas in which people could get lost. In finding their way out visitors would most likely read what the maze had to say and thus digest some of the concepts. LED lights placed on the floor, one to a letter, emitted a series of changing colors setting different moods and enlivening the space. The changing tones afforded the installation a sense of motion. This contributed to confusing those wandering around the installation and created a mild feeling of dizziness, thereby establishing a connection with the former fun park.

The installation had an interactive angle too. Visitors were allowed to draw on the letters, writing words within the words and offering their own opinions and ideas regarding the concepts displayed. They could also attach pictures and photographs to the panels. This form of interaction gave visitors the opportunity to participate in creating a final art piece and to admire each other's work and ideas.

Apostrophy's also designed the stage area where, 5 LED screens were erected, and an art gallery where local artists could showcase their work.

Design: Apostrophy's
Client: Tiger Translate Festival
Event date: February 2009
Design director: Pantavit Lawaroungchok
Producer: Sanchai Chotinoppakun
Art director: Kosin Poonkasem
Creative director: Shy Limanon
Project Manager: Vorapong Teerakawongsakul
Project Coordinator: Chalitinee Meko
Photography: Sirichai Luengvisutisiri
Organizer: Momentum co., ldt

SkyArena

Frankfurt, Germany

The 2006 FIFA World Cup in Germany was a unique media event. For cities like Frankfurt am Main, which hosted four matches, it was also a huge PR opportunity. Frankfurt wanted fans from Germany and elsewhere to see it for what it is: a "modern metropolis" at the very heart of Europe. This called for a spectacular, large-scale event that could generate images powerful enough to travel the entire planet. The goal was to communicate Frankfurt as a vibrant business and cultural center and a likeable, cosmopolitan host, thereby enhancing its image substantially at home and abroad.

A 45-minute light and media show transformed the city skyline into an out-size stage for football images that traveled the world. A dazzling cavalcade of over 500 pictures, projected onto eight high-rise banks, took spectators on an eleven-stage journey through football's great emotions, accompanied by a specially-composed soundtrack. The eleven acts showed eleven great emotions of football: ambition, rise, roughness, respect, joy, mania, pride, hope, sorrow, euphoria and happiness. The images were chosen out of 15,000 pictures from 50 years of football coverage. Atelier Markgraph masterminded the event, who specialize in three-dimensional communication, and design brand and theme events all over the world.

A simple, yet effective technique brought the original still photos to life: the slides moved through the projectors on celluloid strips to create a lateral sense of movement reminiscent of the movies. With an average of four large-scale projectors per slide, cross-fades between images were also possible. In the finished projections, the buildings themselves appeared to interact, with passes flying to and fro and crowds of fans appearing to walk through the picture. To convey more of the pace of football, images burst to life abruptly, then faded to make way for new ones. An original soundtrack by the Frankfurt composer Parviz Mir-Ali added to the sense of drama.

Client: Tourismus + Congress GmbH Frankfurt am Main
Idea, Concept and Production: Atelier Markgraph GmbH (AM)
Creative Direction: Roland Lambrette (AM), Stefan Weil (AM)
Art Direction: Alexander Hanowski (AM)
Project Management: Isa Rekkab (AM)
Direction: Titus Georgi, Philipp Stölzl
Lighting Design: Gunther Hecker
Sound Design: Parviz Mir-Ali
Motion Design and Picture Editing: mbox, Martin Retschitzegger, Maria Johanna Ochsenhofer, Markus Egerter, Holger Mayer
Production of Graphics: Zinnecker-Werberstudio GmbH
Media Technology: XXL-Vision Medientechnik GmbH
Sound Technology: Media Spektrum GmbH & Co. KG
Lighting Technology: Satis&Fy AGDeutschland
Broadcasting and Radio: MM Communications
Construction: Nüssli (Deutschland) GmbH
Industrial Climbers: Marburger Dienstleistungen/ Kletter-Spezial-Einheit
Production of the Soundtrack: Meirelli O.S.T. GmbH
Recording: hr-Sinfonieorchester, hr-Bigband

SkyArena covered a total of 10 000 sqm (108 000 sqft) of the city skyline, so the projections were visible for miles around. Single pictures could be anything up to 1600 sqm large (17 000 sqft). Some 20 km (12 miles) of cable connected the projection areas, loudspeakers and sound systems to ensure perfect audio and video quality. A large team were involved on site to make the show happen, including 40 industrial climbers who used sheets of a special film to turn the buildings into gigantic projector screens.

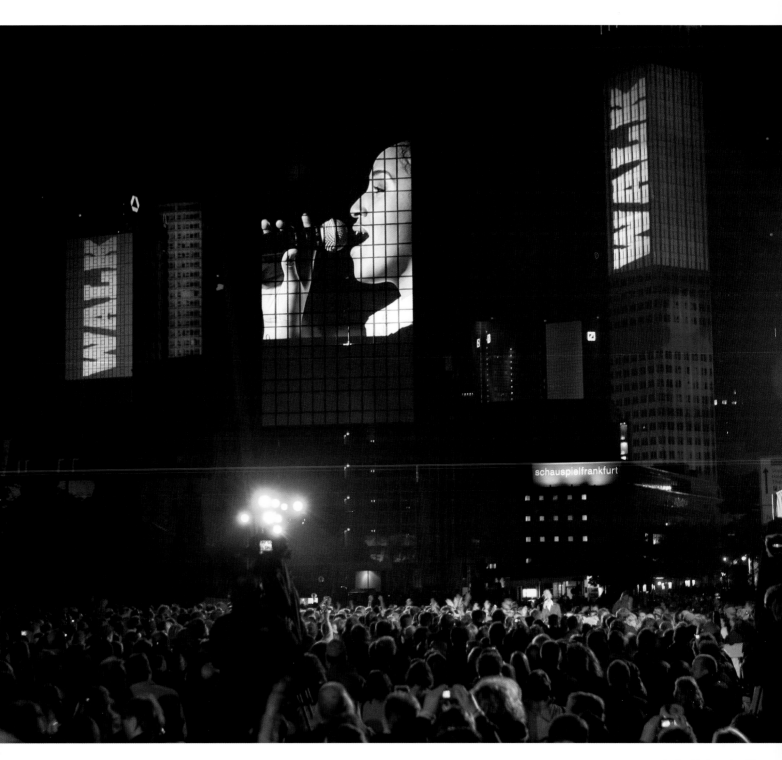

Roche Open Days

Basel, Switzerland

In 2006, the Basel pharmaceutical and diagnostic company, Roche, opened its door to the public with four exhibitions on the topics of "Diabetes", "The journey from an idea to medication", "Medicine of the future" and "Hepatitis and HIV/AIDS" together with an extensive accompanying program. The task of Bellprat Associates was to adapt the scientific content of these four exhibitions in a meaningful manner and to implement it creatively. The public event was aimed at a broad audience with differing needs. The general communication task was to convey Roche's professionalism and expertise and to portray complex, scientific contents in a graphic and stimulating style, appealing both to families and scientists. The two-day event, under the motto "traditional and trailblazing", was intended to create a memorable experience that would remain fresh in visitors' minds for a long time to come.

In order to achieve a three-dimensional event communication, a media mix consisting of five message formats was employed. Scenographic major presentations formed visual icons, leaving long-lasting memories with the visitors and conveying a message on an emotional level. Science shows displayed theatrically prepared contents while offering entertainment and information to a wide audience. Interactive exhibits triggered a process of understanding by observing phenomena. Roche experts demonstrated exhibits, gave brief lectures and answered visitors' questions. Finally, film, image and graphics provided the option to delve deeper into the subject matter.

For the major presentations, it was necessary to reduce complex subjects to a core statement in order to achieve sustainability. "Diabetes" was scenographically reduced to the core statement "Diabetes is about sugar in the blood". White, crystal-like folding objects – symbols for sugar in the blood – formed the core element of the presentation. As a metaphor for blood, the floor and surrounding buildings were shrouded in red material.

The complex "journey from an idea to medication" was scenographically presented as a route comprising various stations. With the aid of large, sometimes walk-in dioramas, each station provided an insight into the research or production processes. A ball track was installed to link the individual stations. The rolling balls symbolized the molecules that continuously decline in numbers in the course of the testing processes, since only the effective molecules go through from the first to the last station.

Design: Bellprat Associates
Client: Roche
Photographs: Contributed by Bellprat Associates

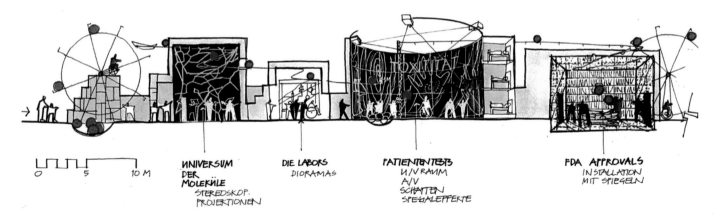

UNIVERSUM
DER
MOLEKÜLE
STEREDSKOP.
PROJEKTIONEN

DIE LABORS
DIORAMAS

PATIENTENTESTS
U/V RAUM
A/V
SCHATTEN
SPEZIALEFFEKTE

FDA APPROVALS
INSTALLATION
MIT SPIEGELN

0   5   10 M

The "Medicine of the future" section was implemented as a science show in an endless loop. Many short dialogue scenes depicted a discussion between a pregnant researcher and a medical layperson. A visionary room appearance was created using neon installations, projections and their reflection in water.

Ball track symbolized the molecules in the complex production process.

PRODUKTION
NEBELRAUM
LABYRINTH
SOUNDSCAPE

GALERIK
GROSSOBJEKTE
OFFENE KARTONS
BILD / TEXT / A/V

DIE ENDPRODUKTE
KARTONSTAPEL
TEXT / GRAFIK

In the "Hepatitis & HIV/AIDS" area, a seemingly infinite mirrored room containing viruses portrayed by green, floating balls was created. Questions could be seen on the spherical viruses from some way off. These, however, could only be read by pulling a ball down by the string. The corresponding answer was written on pillars below each ball.

HUGO BOSS Fashion Show

Metzingen, Germany

Publicmotor together with German architecture firm Bottega + Ehrhardt Architekten provided the structure that would present the Hugo Boss Fall/ Winter 2008 collection to an international audience of more than 1,000 guests. The event took place in Metzingen, a small town close to Stuttgart, where the headquarters of Hugo Boss is located.

The huge tent was built as an ephemeral structure with a surface area of about 60 x 60m (200 x 200ft), and was transformed into a homogeneously red and black colored event space. The floor plan was subdivided into four programmatic zones; the entrance zone, the main party zone, the fashion show zone and the backstage zone. Guests entered through two entrances, connected to a huge cloakroom and through illuminated black corridors with small vertical openings towards the main space. A huge red bar, illuminated by suspended theatre spotlights, creating abstract chandeliers and ornamental shadows on the back wall, was used to serve the welcome drinks. A red funnel-shaped entrance led to the fashion show zone with a shiny white catwalk in the center of two black tribunes. The models entered the catwalk through a shiny black funnel, reflecting themselves and the white line of the catwalk.

After the fashion show the lounge area became the center of the event, separated by a curtain of suspended black Plexiglas stripes. Dark wooden volumes in different heights, either to stand or sit at, a dance floor in the center and an artificial starry sky made from individual light bulbs created a lively lounge atmosphere. While drinks were served again on the central red bar by black dressed bartenders, the food was served by white dressed cooks on two red counters, located sideways. The clearly structured event architecture underscored the uncompromisingly stylish fashion of Hugo Boss.

Architects: Bottega + Ehrhardt Architekten, GmbH
Giorgio Bottega, Henning Ehrhardt, Christoph Seebald
Collaborator: Philip Jin Honermann
Event Design/Management: PUBLICMOTOR Brand Communication, Nico Hofmann
Collaborators: Helene Berg
Client: HUGO BOSS AG
Photographs: Axel Schultz, Stuttgart

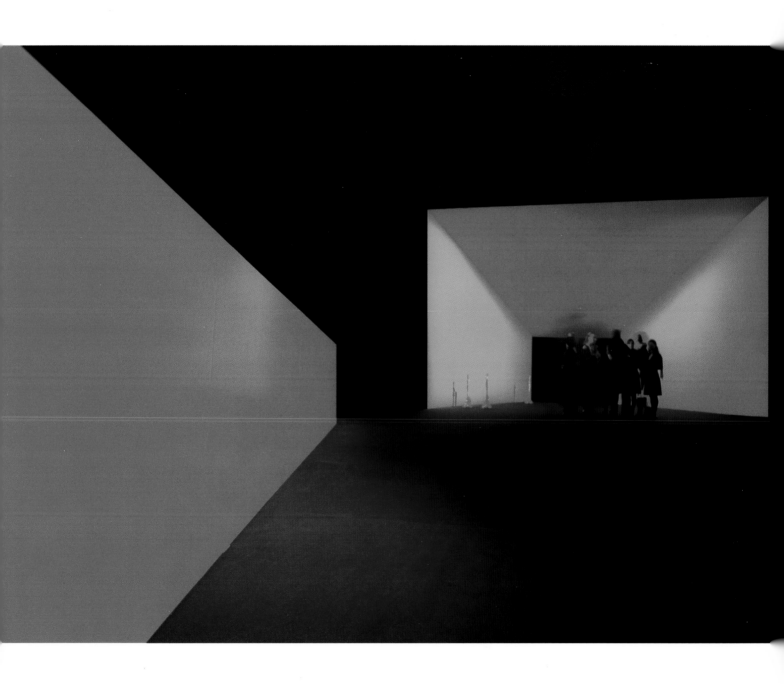

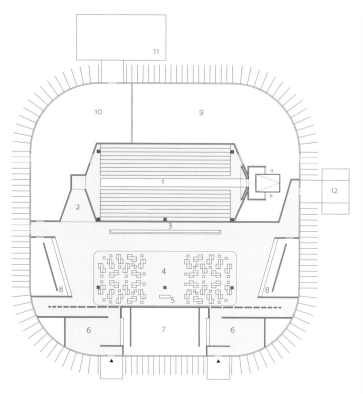

1. Catwalk
2. Entrance Fashion Show
3. Bar
4. Lounge
5. Discjockey
6. Entrance

7. Cloakroom
8. Catering
9. Backstage Models
10. Backstage Catering / Enigneering
11. Kitchen
12. Restrooms

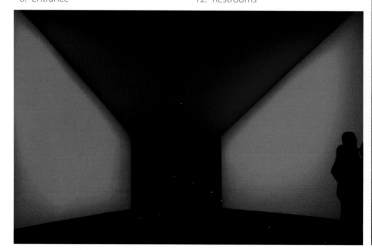

Ohel

Warsaw, Poland

The Hebrew word ohel has a variety of meanings in Jewish culture which could be appropriate to this space. Firstly it means a tent or a home; secondly a house of study (sometimes used for names of synagogues) and thirdly it is used to describe the structures built over the graves of important figures in Jewish culture, such as rabbis.

It symbolizes bringing people together. This ohel in Warsaw is a temporary artistic installation, constructed on the site of what is to be the public space and structure of the future Museum of the History of Polish Jews in Warsaw. The main idea of the pavilion is to promote the museum, informing visitors through a range of different media about its successive construction stages. The 95 sqm (1000 sqft) space under the roof serves as a temporary forum for presentations, thought exchange and discussions. As an active educational and cultural center for the local community and inhabitants of Warsaw, Ohel places special emphasis on the education of young people. The shape and role of the tent corresponds to what is to be the future main lobby of the museum building.

The Ohel pavilion is a temporary folding textile structure and measures 18 x 18 x 5 m (60 x 60 x 16 ft). It consists of a polyester envelope in blue PCV pitched on a steel structure made from scaffolding. Such a design enables the tent to be easily dismantled and reconstructed in another location. The blue tunnel has a wide, 4.5m (14.7 ft) high mouth, which acts as the main entrance and narrows down to a smaller opening at the back. Its sinuous curves and organic form affords the structure a humanized aesthetic, which connects with its purpose. Part of the designers' vision is for the pavilion to be built on several of Warsaw's main squares.

After the museum is finished the mobile structure will play a role as an information and promotional desk, which can travel across the world. The tent provides an area for exhibitions as well as large screen presentations and lectures, concerts and press conferences. According to the design concept the pavilion is able to withstand weather conditions in all seasons.

Design: Centrala (Małgorzata Kuciewicz, Krzysztof Banaszewski and Jakub Szczęsny) in cooperation with Dominik Strzelec
Client: Museum of the History of Polish Jews
Surface area: 95 sqm (1000 sqft)
Completion: May 2006
Photographs: contributed by Centrala

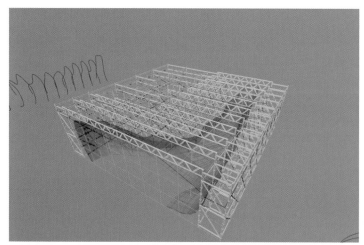

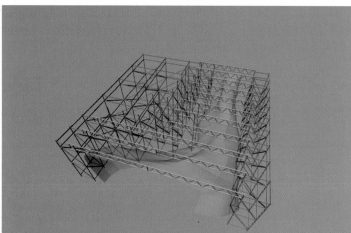

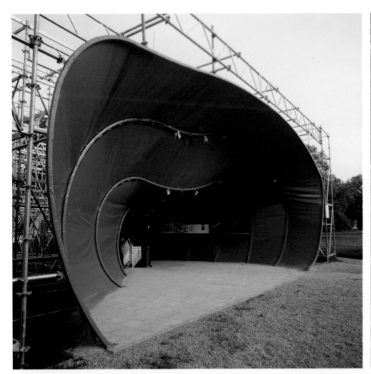

BASF pack.it.2006

Ludwigshafen, Germany

Packaging is an indispensable covering for most things in life, and simultaneously conceals its own inner values – the materials to which it owes the variety of its formal and functional options. BASF pack.it.2006 revealed this link and provided a glimpse of the fascinating packaging possibilities of the future. One hundred leading representatives of the packaging and branded goods industry experienced an event designed and implemented by circ; the event itself was transformed into packaging, interpreting the expertise of BASF in packaging informatively, interactively, culturally and culinarily. The event venue at the BASF Gesellschaftshaus in Ludwigshafen welcomed participants in a fascinating wrapping and gave an impressive demonstration of what packaging can achieve when the power of design is united with the capabilities of the material. 5,000 sqm (53,800 sqft) of aluminum-coated polyamide fabric clothed the Wilhelminian building like a second skin and extended to the surrounding trees as well as the interior of the building. "La Réflexion du Fond" is a work of the French artist Xavier Juillot, who used a special low-pressure technology for it: air ducts below the building wrapping facilitated the visual impression of a breathing organism.

Design: circ gmbh & co. kg
Client: BASF SE
Photographs: contributed by circ

District @ Amsterdam International Fashion Week

Amsterdam, The Netherlands

Moshi Moshi is a new luxury fashion group based in Amsterdam. Each year the group organizes the Amsterdam International Fashion Week (AIFW) and District, an initiative started by the firm as an attempt to put the Dutch capital on the map as an international destination for fashion, in particularly for the growing new luxury segment. Local design studio Concrete Architectural Associates was commissioned by Moshi Moshi for the concept of the design for the event. The goal was to create a unique event, which dissociated itself from the standard fashion show format. In cooperation with District, Concrete's intention was to create a fair which resembled "a good night out full of excitement, where visitors would lose track of time."

The grounds of the 2005 edition of AIFW were divided into three areas. The Transformator building was adjusted to be able to host catwalk shows, the Gasthouder (fair) was designed to accommodate approximately 100 brands and the Pavilion was created to accommodate the lounge area and the parties. The pavilion was also the connection between the Gasthouder and the Transformator building, so the guests could visit all areas without getting cold, since this was the winter edition of the event and took place in January.

In the pavilion the entranceway and corridors were left untreated, which served to highlight the luxurious pink carpet that was placed on the floor in the lounge.

The Gasthouder consisted of 58 cylindrical stands with 5 different diameters. The cylinders were formed by white semi-transparent curtains hanging from trusses (circular steel bars) from the ceiling. Clothing racks were placed in every stand, which had the same bending radius as the trusses that form the stand. The semi-transparent curtains triggered curiosity and revealed brands, which were unknown to many of the attendees. The floor of the Gasthouder was left untreated, but each stand had it's own round wooden floor made of okoume multi-ply board. The walls and the ceiling were left in their original state, like in the pavilion. In the middle of the fair a big cylinder was built from white curtains and a wooden floor to provide an area for the restaurant. A pink, comfortable, leather couch was placed along the edges of the stand, and a round bar presided over the middle of the restaurant. Finally the smallest stand close to the restaurant was reserved for a DJ.

Design: Concrete Architectural Associates
Project team: Rob Wagemans, Jan Paul Scholtmeijer, Stan Flohr
General contractor: PTB, Partner in Building
Tent: Neptunus Structures
Client: Moshi Moshi
Photographs: Jeroen Musch

On their way to the lounge visitors passed the reception desk, a multi-ply cylindrical bar with a pink leather top. White curtains made from cheesecloth, a light woven fabric, were draped vertically along the walls in the lounge, and then gathered towards the middle of the ceiling. A chandelier with a radius of 8 m (26 ft) hung from the center of the ceiling, which in combination with a selection of moving heads provided an attractive light for the lounge.

eKTOP-1

Paris, France

Nuit blanche is a highly popular, all-night cultural festival that takes place once a year in the middle of Paris. The exyzt design team was asked by the event organizers to create an installation that would generate curiosity among the festival goers and attract their attention.

eKTOP-1 was an enormous incongruous structure placed in the Jardin des Halles in central Paris, where thousands of tourists and locals alike were drawn by its bizarre appearance. The structure was intended to resemble a satellite, which was floating through the square. It was a lightweight structure with a white fabric skin, supported by a massive framework of scaffolding.

The satellite contained hidden cameras that filmed those who approached. The films were shown live on the wall of one of the buildings that stood in front of the structure, thereby allowing everyone to see how people were reacting to the installation. The idea was one of irony: those who stopped to look at the installation were, in fact, being looked at by the installation. Spotlights were also employed that followed visitors across the square, enhancing the general feeling that the satellite was spying on its surroundings.

Later on during the night flashing lights behind the satellite's skin combined with live music to create a spectacular sound and light show, performed by the 'crew' of the bizarre spacecraft. Shadows of guitarists and other performers could be seen from the outside enhancing the effect of the installation.

Design: Exyzt
Client: Nuit Blanch
Photographs: contruibuted by Exyzt

MotoPEBL

Hamburg, Germany

Berlin based, visual communications agency flora&faunavisions turned the July 2006 press launch of Motorola's new PEBL Color device into a bright and beautiful design extravaganza by adding a glorious splash of color to Hamburg's city center.

Based on the brand's global "City Strips" theme – composed of the phones' four distinct color options – the ffv design team translated the original 2D strip motif created by the international lead agency The Fish Can Sing to the three dimensional realm of Hamburg's Kunsthalle.

Perfectly molded to the art gallery's expansive forecourt, huge patterns of glorious PEBL stripes provided a classy, timeless, yet abstract allusion to the phone's smooth and elegant curves. Printed on several pieces of water-proof, durable vinyl and covering around 250 sqm (2690 sqft), it took a team of 10 technicians to assemble the resulting pattern from its individual, pre-plotted jigsaw pieces.

Akin to walkable "guide-lines," these color-coded stripes and swirls piqued the imagination of VIPs and public alike, leading invited guests to the event held at the museum's spectacular atrium, fitted with a special 360 degree video installation composed of eight individual projectors.

Here, and in the stylish bistro, 250 guests enjoyed a further multi-sensory variant of the PEBL's characteristic color spectrum. Surrounded by thin bands of PEBL phones, strung up like glistening pearl necklaces, and illuminated by a lighting installation that transformed the double-glazed windows into giant light boxes, their taste buds were treated to a four-course flying buffet based on the brand's distinct color scheme, finishing off with a burst of bright orange.

Deceptively simple, yet immaculately sculpted and designed, the result created a colorful, immediate and memorable event

Design and production: flora&faunavisions
Client: Motorola GmbH, executed by Markus Friedrichs (Marketing, Germany)
Lead agency international: The Fish Can Sing LTD
Photographs: contributed by flora&faunavisions, die photodesigner.de

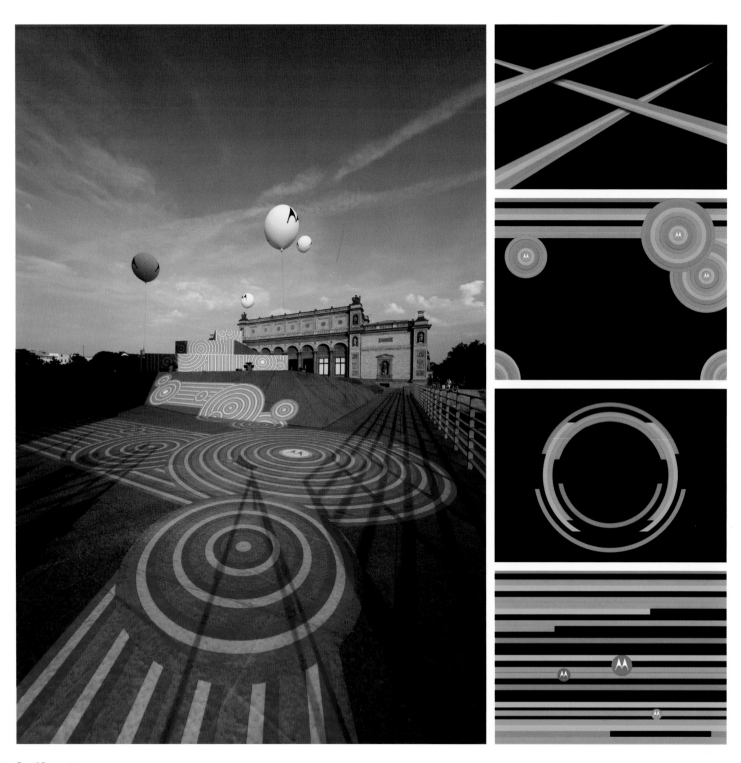

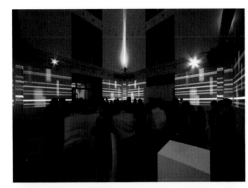

Opposite page: Video stills with the Motorola "City Strips" theme.
This page: images of the event.

Motorola SLVR

Berlin, Germany

Mobile phone specialist Motorola commissioned flora&faunavisions to put together an event that would introduce its new, slim flagship model, the SLVR, to the German public as part of a global launch campaign. To unveil this svelte creation in style, the visual communications team created a PR event based on the device's deceptively clever juxtaposition of wafer-thin elegance and full-featured functionality. For this event what you saw is not what you got – an optical illusion picked up and spun out by flora&faunavisions.

The launch played on varying sets of binaries: slim and chunky, urban and edgy, indoors and outdoors, encompassing both East Berlin's landmark square, the Alexanderplatz, bathed in a stark set of Blade Runner-esque visuals, and an exclusive indoor location at sleek and chic hotspot Shiro I Shiro. This would be the first ever event to take place at this new restaurant and boutique hotel, and flora&faunavisions took advantage of Shiro I Shiro's pre-opening state and requisitioned several still-empty rooms for technical back up and projector positioning.

For the indoor PR part of the launch, the restaurant's sharp, modern austerity emphasized and accentuated the SLVR's basic geometric shapes, de- and reconstructed in an image trailer and projections interspersed with various electrifying shades of blue. From Perspex earrings to angular ties, even the outfits and accessories picked up on the product's "slimmer than ever" theme.

Introducing the phone itself and triggered by each press of a SLVR button, Motorola's Head of Mobile Devices launched the outdoor part of the evening with a series of giant Pani slide and laser projections. For a few precious hours, these monochrome, high-contrast images – optimized for projection on mirrored glass façades – bathed seven of the square's most prominent buildings in the stark, ghostly aesthetics of a modern-day Gotham City, including a full-format projection on the square's Park Inn Hotel, topped by a green laser tracing of the phone itself.

Design and production: flora&faunavisions
Client: Motorola GmbH, Markus Friedrichs, die photodesigner.de
Lead agency international: Cake Group, London
Photographs: contributed by flora&faunavisions, die photodesigner.de

Images of the projections in Alexanderplatz.

Images of the event in Shiro I Shiro and stills from the projections used there.

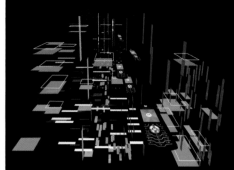

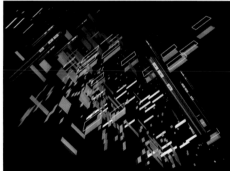

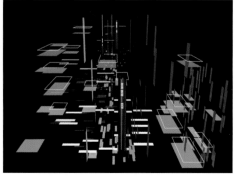

Land Rover Sculpture

Goodwood, UK

Designed and produced by Gerry Judah, engineered by Capita Bobrowski and constructed by Littlehampton Welding Ltd., the Land Rover Sculpture for the Goodwood Festival of Speed 2008 celebrates the marque's 60 years. Consisting of 3,415 sections of steel weighing 120 tonnes, the "Rock" displays five vehicles that appear to be driving over its rough and undulated terrain. The sculpture was also designed as an open grid structure to enable visitors at Goodwood House to be able to see through it to the events within the Festival of Speed as well as allow the visitors from the event to see the house. An added attraction of the sculpture consisted of an open interior space allowing spectacular views of the sculpture from within.

Design & production: Gerry Judah
Engineering: Capita Bobrowski
Construction: Littlehampton Welding Ltd.
Client: Land Rover
Photographs: contributed by Gerry Judah

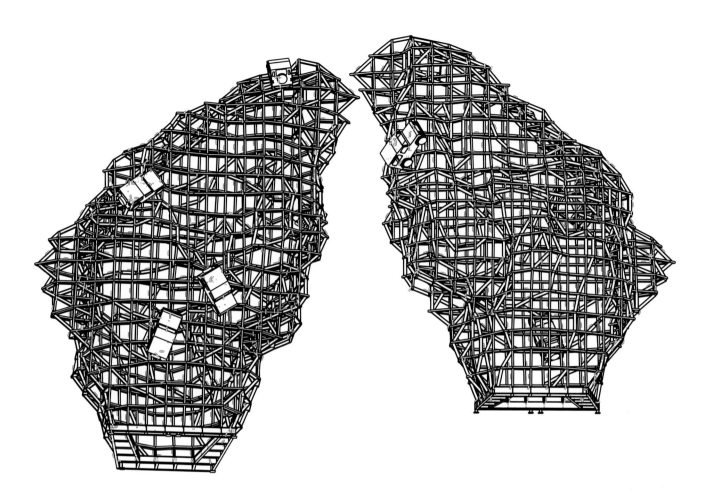

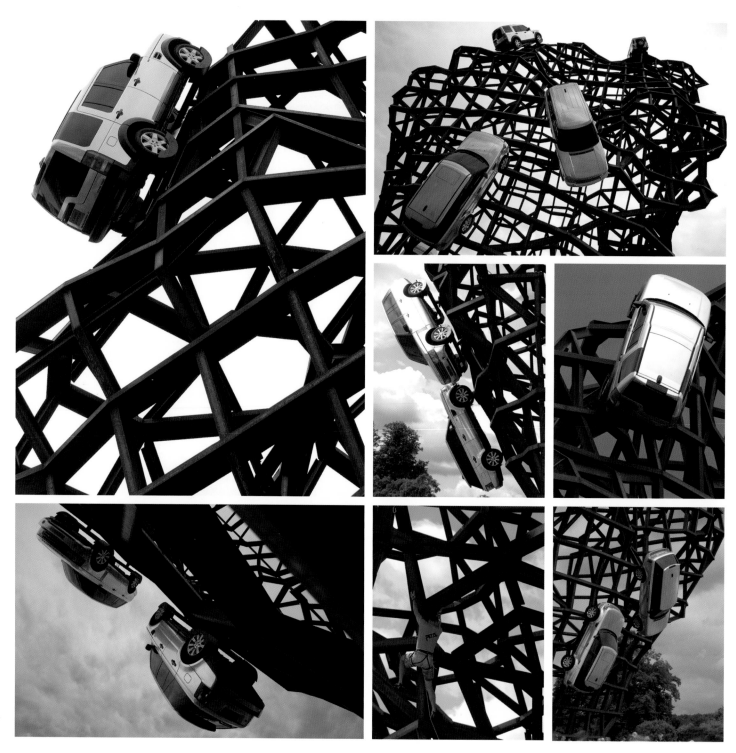

Toyota Sculpture

Goodwood, UK

Designed and produced by Gerry Judah, engineered by Capita Bobrowski and constructed by Littlehampton Welding Ltd., the Toyota Sculpture for the Goodwood Festival of Speed 2007 celebrates the marque's history with a Japanese theme. A series of 26 m (85 ft) high to 38 m (125 ft) high "Torri" gates create a promenade from the racetrack towards Goodwood House. Suspended within the gates are a series of historic racing cars tethered to the structure in a curved movement allowing dramatic views of the vehicles from all directions. With the use of tensioned Mackeloid steel rods, each car supports the structure as much as the structure supports the cars.

Design & production : Gerry Judah
Engineering: Capita Bobrowski
Construction: Littlehampton Welding Ltd.
Client: Toyota
Photographs: contributed by Gerry Judah

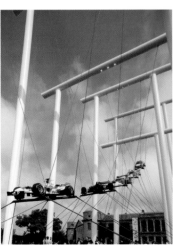

Open Burble

Singapore

Open Burble has developed from a project originally commissioned for the Singapore Biennial 2006, called Open Burble. The Burble is a massive, 70 m (230 ft) tall structure reaching up towards the sky, composed of approximately 1000 extra-large helium balloons each of which contains micro-controllers and LEDs that create spectacular patterns of light across the surface of the structure. The balloons are supported by 140 carbon-fiber hexagonal units.

The public, both audience and performer, come together to control this immense rippling, glowing, bustling 'Burble' that sways in the evening sky, in response to movements of the long articulated interactive handle bar at the base of the structure. The ephemeral experience exists on such a large scale that it is able to compete visually in an urban context with the buildings that surround it.

The Burble is held down to the ground by the combined weight of the crowds holding on to the handle bar. They may position it as they like. They may curve in on themselves, or pull it in a straight line - the form is a combination of the crowd's desires and the impact of wind currents varying throughout the height of the Burble.

As people on the ground shake and pump the handle bars of the Burble, they see their movements echoed as colors through the entire system. Part installation, part performance, the Burble enables people to contribute on an urban scale to a structure that occupies their city, albeit for only one night.

Open Burble is a real interactive experience, rather than a virtual one, with a wonderful sense of collectiveness and optimism about it. Its understated simplicity is supported by a complex design and production process that embrace the high and low-tech to great effect

Design: Haque Design + Research
Core team: Usman Haque (architect),
Rolf Pixley (algorithmist and chromodynamicist),
Barbara Jasinowicz (production supervisor),
Ivan Roncari (assembly supervisor),
Seth Garlock (B2B network, balloon hardware design),
Ai Hasegawa (general fabrication),
Mo-Ling Chui (project liaison)
Handle bar design, fabrication, testing, field operations: Toby Carr, Richard Grimes, Fred Guttfield, Elliot Payne.
Fabrication and field operations: Alex, Marta, Genevieve, Carlos, Letizia, Momoe, Abdelwahid Bachiri, Chao Rong Chen, Susan Haque, John Jorgensen, Graham Northmore, Hiromi Ozaki, Madalina Pierseca, Karen Silvia Mendoza Pinto, Vasile Radu, Thomas Thwaites, Seok Hwan Yang.
Site assembly: 27 people from Affinity Crew and Moet, co-ordinated by Rachel King.
Security and electronics rescue: Cosmo, Sheldon and 4 others.
And thanks for emergency help when the wind picked up: Ruairi Glynn, Christian Kerrigan, Shane Solanki, and a couple of hundred Londoners.
Photographs: Eng Kiat Tan / Haque Design + Research Ltd

Exhibition Furniture

London Festival of Architecture 2008, London, UK

The project was for a number of pieces of exhibition furniture placed across London as part of the core program for the London Festival of Architecture 2008. The exhibition furniture consists of plywood cut-out versions of a sofa, armchair, bookshelf and enormous lamps. These domestic objects are adorned with a pattern designed by London-based global fashion and design company Eley Kishimoto in the Festival's signature pink.

The first home of the furniture was all together in the Somerset House courtyard as part of "London's Largest Living Room" for the launch of the festival. Jointly produced by Design for London and the London Festival of Architecture, and with creative direction by Gerrard O'Carroll, London's Largest Living Room invited members of the public to think about the city landscape as their home, and consider how we could better use the often neglected open spaces around us. The second homes of the furniture were in various parks and public spaces across the capital where they stayed for the remainder of the festival before being adopted by a number of galleries, public spaces, and individuals. The sofas also carried an exhibition of location-specific writing contributed by the teachers and students of the History, Theory, and Interpretation MA at London Metropolitan University. These "nuggets" of information invited visitors to take a fresh look at the view around them as they took a seat in one of the large outdoor sofas or armchairs. The furniture was designed to resemble flat-pack versions of antique furniture. To achieve this, the designers thought of the components of the furniture: the back, front, seat, arms; as elevations and plans of the flamboyant furniture that were to be emulated. CNC (computer numerical control) technology was used to quickly and accurately cut the plywood out into its flat-pack components. Tabs, like those in toy models and dolls' house furniture, were used to allow simple and precise assembly. The tabs also added to the playfulness and slightly odd sense of scale. The furniture was made from 1525 x 3050 x 24mm thick birch plywood panels, and designed taking this size limit into account. This also ensured that the individual pieces could be handled with relative ease as the furniture needed to be easy to assemble and disassemble as it traveled to its various locations. The pink pattern was silk-screen printed directly onto the plywood which was then CNC routed into the component pieces. These pieces were treated with wood preserver to prevent rot and fungus, and finished with a clear varnish.

Design: Studio Weave & Studio Myerscough
Client: Design for London/
London Festival of Architecture
Creative direction: Gerrard O'Carroll
Carpet design: Morag Myerscough/
Studio Myerscough
Furniture: Studio Weave
with a pattern printed on it by Eley Kishimoto
Photographs: Studio Weave & Studio Myerscough

© Studio Weave ▶

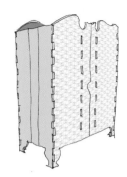

All items were silk-screened with a pattern elaborated by fashion and design company Eley Kishimoto in the festival's signature pink.

Commencement Ceremony

Philadelphia, Pennsylvania, USA

The University of Pennsylvania decided to redesign their annual Commencement Weekend ceremony, re-energizing a program that had become inefficient and had lost an aesthetic focus. The traditional site is Franklin Field, an historic stadium within the campus, with space for events. The project was to reconsider the presentation of the ceremony, to be both inspirational and practical for the 20 000 guests, 5000 students, and faculty and honorees. MGA Partners was responsible for all aspects of the design and documentation of the custom canopy structure; stage; scene; and seating platform. The firm also directed procession choreography and seating layouts; lectern; program artwork; and large-scale printed fabric graphics.

Years past, when trustees, alumni, faculty, administration, and students made their exuberant procession across the campus to Franklin Field, they stopped at the gates. Now the choreography of the event extends to their destination, as the long colorful line of people passes onto the field and through the stage portal to greet their guests and take their seats.

The challenge was to generate enthusiasm and participation from 15-20,000 guests in a stadium with a much larger seating capacity. The new stage subdivides the vast space of Franklin Field, concentrating the guests in the closed end to create an arena environment. The orientation is west - to the familiar towers of the University in the background, a reminder of this time of transition for the new graduates.

As a designed object, the stage presents a focus for the excitement of the day. The flaring canopy rises from the middle of the stage acting as a mediator of scale between the stadium and the university president, distinguished speakers, and honorees who stand at the podium. The set is an integrated surface of translucent graphic textiles, with giant video screens mounted at each end of the scaffolding that transmit the content and drama of the ceremony to everyone in the stands.

Architects: MGA Partners Architects
Client: University of Pennsylvania
Photographs: Barry Halkin

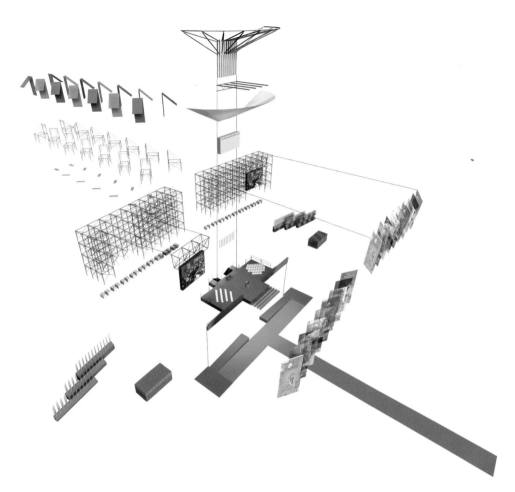

The architecture is temporary because it is erected for a single event; however, it is not disposable. This project is designed as a kit of parts to be re-used for many years. For the University, it is a practical economic choice in lieu of rented tents, throwaway carpentry, and multiple vendors. Tectonically, the stage, the scene, and the canopy are a construction of standard and custom steel components designed to be easily assembled and structurally independent of the synthetic turf field.

Kiss The Frog!

Oslo, Norway

The backdrop to this project is the merging of four museums, considered by some to be very different to one another. The National Gallery, The Museum of Decorative Arts and Design, The Norwegian Museum of Architecture and The National Museum of Contemporary Art is now The New National Museum of Art, Architecture and Design. Kiss The Frog! Is both a celebration of the new museum and the first project to manifest its ambitions for the future, exploring the aesthetics of transformation, referring to genre transcendence both as method, expression and experience. It also marks Norway's 100-year anniversary as a free nation.

The concept for the temporary art pavilion is based on the fairytale cliché, in which a beautiful, rich prince suffers an evil spell and is consequently trapped within the shape of a frog. One day, when a princess kisses him, he is transformed back to the prince he really is, and they live happily ever after. With its organic shape the frog can be seen as an embodiment of the museums' transformation, representing the ongoing reinterpretation of interdisciplinary art and challenging the boundaries between art, architecture, design and popular culture. It is also a mediator between the past and the future, connecting the old National Gallery and the new Art Hall.

Kiss The Frog! is a 1500 sqm (16100 sqft) pneumatic textile structure. Based on the principles of a zeppelin, the weatherproof nylon fabric is kept up by the difference in air-pressure between inside and outside. A huge fan constantly supplies the inside of the pavilion with fresh air, which is then trapped inside the frog and maintains it inflated. The frog has no straight edges or lines, only curved walls smoothly transcending into a roof, and then to a wall again. A series of circular sections forms a path or walkway inside the structure. The fabric is supported by seven arches of circle shaped beams, evenly spread along the interior walkway.

Design: MMW Architects of Norway
Principal Architect: Sindre Østereng & Magne Magler Wiggen
Collaborator: Rebekka Bondesen, Eirik Førde, Helle Gundersen, Hallstein Guthu, Svein Hertel-Aas, Jon Arne Jørgensen, Siri Sverdrup Liset, Virginie Mira, Kathrine Nyquist, Sindre Østereng
Structural Engineering: Dr. Techn. Kristoffer Apeland AS by Kristoffer Apeland, Agatha Alsadi and Rolf Smetveit . Buro Happold by Steven Brown
Contractor: Hallmaker as, Graboplan AB
Client: The National Museum of Art, Architecture and Design
Photographs: Jiri Havran, Eirik Foerde, Martin Sunde Skulstad

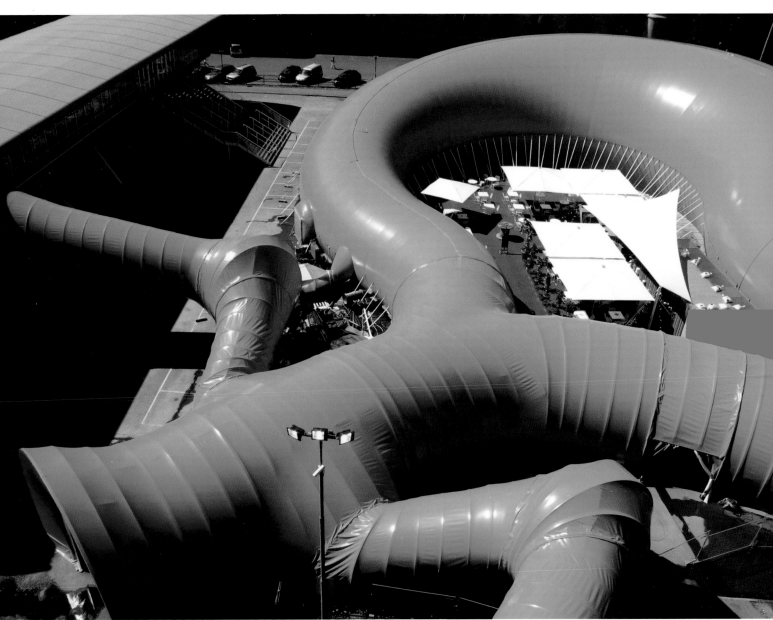

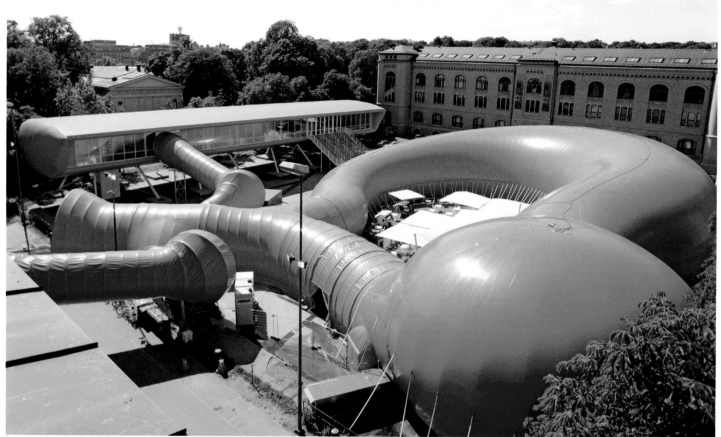

The entrance is through what appears to be the mouth of the frog opposite which is the reception. To the right it is possible to enter the old National Gallery through one of the legs and through the window taken out for this occasion. To the left is the other frog leg enclosing another staircase, which leads to the entrance of the semi-permanent pavilion. Behind the reception a pair of revolving doors allows visitors to go inside. These doors were chosen for their ability to fuse visitors in and out and thus avoid decreasing the frog's pressure.

© mmw.no > photo: Eirik Foerde

© mmw.no > photo: Martin Sunde Skulstad

© mmw.no > photo: Eirik Foerde

© mmw.no > photo: Martin Sunde Skulstad

© mmw.no > photo: Eirik Foerde

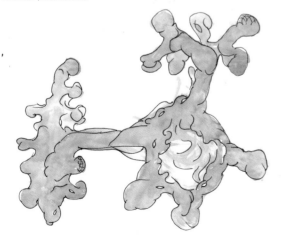

Because of the curved sections there are no straight walls to attach pieces of art to. The artists were therefore required to make their own freestanding installations dedicated to the discussion of historical and contemporary art. Several of the artists worked with large installations and projects, which commented on the borders (or non-borders) between art, design and architecture. All of the pieces were made specifically for this occasion - the kissing of the frog.

© mmw.no > photo: Eirik Foerde

In the center of the shape is an open space for stage activities and dining, where there are seats for 150 people in front of a 60 sqm (645 sqft) stage space.

© mmw.no > photo: Eirik Foerde

Pink project

New Orleans, Louisiana, USA

The Lower Ninth Ward, a rich cultural community long known for its high proportion of resident ownership, was left devastated and homeless in the wake of Hurricane Katrina. Unfortunately to date, initiatives to rebuild this once vibrant area have fallen short. As a catalyst for positive change, the Pink Project rallies for opportunities hidden within this tragedy.

Pink, as the inaugural event for the Make It Right initiative, refocuses attention onto the plight of the Lower Ninth, this time with optimism and purpose: Pink is the virtual city of Hope. A hybrid of art, architecture, cinema, media and fundraising strategies, Pink is concieved as an informational commemorative communication tool, which both raises awareness and activates individual participation to heal local wounds in need of global aid. While filming on set in New Orleans, Brad Pitt, fascinated with the sharp color contrast between a pink CGI set and its lush green surroundings, identified the visual potency of assembling pink houses as a metaphor. Together with GRAFT, the idea was born to merge film and architecture into an installation that would focus immediate global attention onto a pervasive local issue. Filmic concepts drive the narrative of the installation, framing the architectural development. The scenes within the assembly create emotive and informative storyboards containing specific perspectives rich with history and memorialization. It is only over time and through monetary donations that these pink placeholders become reassembled, registering the effects of a collective consiousness in real time, unltimately enabling the construction of 150 real homes. The simple legibility of the pink monopoly house reassembled from smaller individual components intentionally focus attention onto a problematic of manageable scale. Allowing the individual to physically participate with the installation through his or her donations, the web driven fundraising tool bridges the gap between the virtual and the real.

Pink does not dwell on the past but rather empowers the future. Through the immediate potency of the spectacle, aided by local and global media, it attempts to disassociate itself from the negative connotations of that which has failed. Creating a call to action filled with hope and promise, Pink generates an armature robust enough to enable the outpouring of individuals into a collective effort striving for positive change. Reversing the diaspora, bringing people home.

Initiator and Designer: Brad Pitt
Curator: Graft
Partners: Lars Krückeberg, Wolfram Putz, Thomas Willemeit, Alejandra Lillo, Gregor Hoheisel
Team: Mosska Adeil, Celi Freeman, Mick van Gemert, Neiel Norheim, Dirk Pause, Christoph Rauhut, Verena Schreppel, Susanne Woitke, Michael Zach
Executive Producer: Stefan Beese (Graft)
Co Producer: Nina Killeen
Co Producer: Stephen Rehage, Rehage Entertainment
Lighting Designer: Herve Descottes, L'Observatoire International
Project Management: Beatrice Witzgall
Project Support: Oscar Louveau
Renderer: Anna Muslimova
Lighting Design Technicians: Adam Ford and Rendon Slade, Universal
Development & Fabrication: Jay Gernsbacher, Center Staging
Sleeve Fabrication: Anthony Manno, Marine Tops & Covers
Artist: Lionel Milton, Elleone
Videographer: Jason Villemarette and Christopher Whittaker
Photographs: Ricky Ridecos

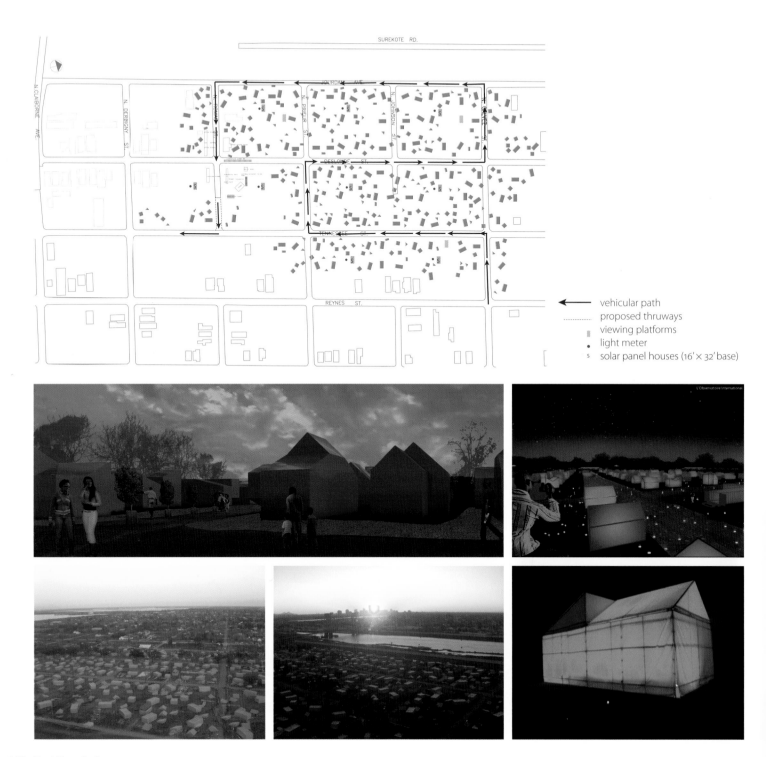

vehicular path
proposed thruways
viewing platforms
light meter
solar panel houses (16' × 32' base)

Taste Lab

Barcelona, Spain

The Taste Lab project explored the relationship between space, volume, transparency and light, fusing all human senses with the sense of taste. The space presented visitors with a high quality gastronomical experience created by Catalunya's world famous gourmet restaurant elBulli.

The project consisted of a large transparent, contained space that was able to create a visual dialogue between the exterior and the interior space that formed the boundary to the project. The elements that form the context of the Olympic Needle in Montjuic (the Olympic Stadium, the Telecommunications Tower and the Palau Sant Jordi) all interacted within the space.

The interior of the space was lit via three luminous prisms of different proportions which, being contained within the transparent space, created a transitional space between the exterior context and the interior. The central prism that comprised the entrance hall led on to two smaller prisms (cloakroom, technical area and toilets) which integrated with one another to create a progression of spaces, thus forming a succession of luminous planes. Visitors crossed the entrance hall and entered a large open-plan, transparent space with a capacity for 350 diners. A multitude of suspended dots of light hung above the tables. Through their reflections on the ceiling the lights multiplied to form an enormous interior constellation.

Design: ex.studio, Patricia Meneses + Iván Juárez
Client: El Bulli Restaurant
Photographs: contributed by ex.studio

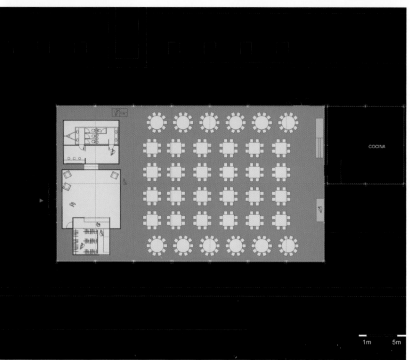

COCINA

1m   5m

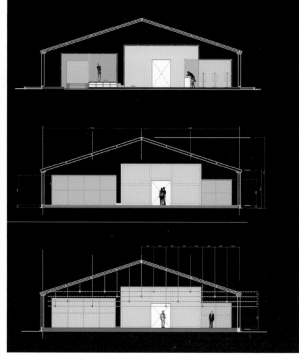

Media Cloud

Seoul, South Korea

Hi Seoul festival is an open-air event held each year at springtime in the Korean capital to celebrate the nation's rich culture and long history. In 2008 the Seoul Foundation for Arts and Culture commissioned Korean architects Mass Studies, with the the spatial design of the festival's central location, the city's Town Hall Square. For the design and development of the design's central piece, the so called media cloud, Mass Studies got realities:united, a German based studio for art and architecture on board.

Shaped like a tornado, the installation developed from a central 'eye', from which it rose and spread outwards. The Media Cloud consisted of an array of 1,265 linear LED units that developed strong centripetal forces 16 m (52 ft) above the festival crowd, changing colors and enlivening the festivities. Short strips of white plastic were attached to each of the LED units, creating comb-like structures that set the whole installation in motion when the wind blew. The steel wire structure was suspended from a total of five steel towers and floated in the center of the large circular plaza. The Cloud measured an impressive 55 m (180 ft) in diameter and took just five days to fully construct.

Framed by Seoul's skyline, this enormous temporary chandelier created the central event space called "May Palace" for the one-week festival program. During the day, set in motion by the wind, the appropriately named Cloud served as protection against the sun, whilst at night an elaborate choreography of animated light patterns swirled above the three main performance stages on Seoul Plaza.

Design: Mass Studies featuring realities:united
Client: Seoul Foundation for Arts and Culture
Date: May 2008
Project manager:
Mass Studies: Joungwon Lee
realities:united: Christoph Wagner
Project team:
Mass Studies: Minsuk Cho, Kisu Park,
Jisoo Kim, Sungpil Won
realities:united: Jan Edler, Malte Niedringhaus,
Wolfgang Metschan, Tim Edler
Collaborators: Alto
Photographs: realities:united

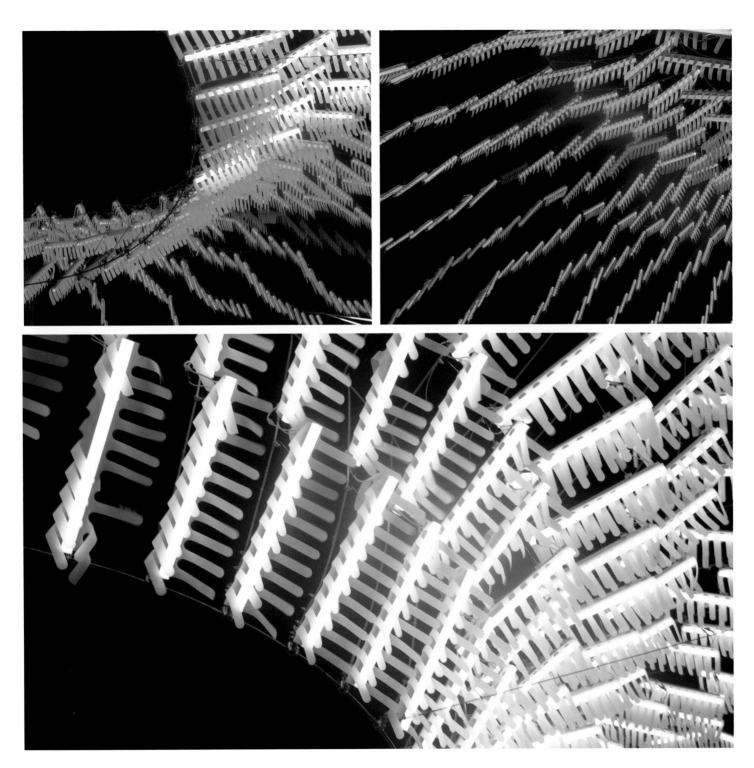

Floating Objects

Kiminomori New Town, Chiba prefecture, Japan

Art Universiade 2002 was an art-related event held across four newly developed towns in the southeast of Japan. Whilst being different in many aspects the four towns all shared the typical characteristics of housing developments that have been carried out in Japan since World War II. A shortage of time and funds has meant these places have developed without the community spirit and warm feel of a naturally evolved town. The Art Universiade was intended to produce projects that could improve the environments in these towns and provide ideas for other such communities.

Ryumei Fujiki decided to create three sub-projects, which would be related to one another through the concept: 'floating objects'. The objective of the project was to shorten the psychological distance between the community and their local golf course, which accounts for roughly half of the town itself.

It was decided that for a single summer a group of sunflowers would float on the pond at the eighth hole of the Kiminomori golf course. These flowers were supported by Styrofoam disks. The intention of the project was to reach out to the community since these installations could be seen from the adjacent Sakura Park.

On the day of a music concert, which was held by the Kiminomori Golf Club, the floating flowers were illuminated with a mystical blue light, creating a dramatic change from the scene portrayed during the day.

The Solar Balloon Experiment was held next to the golf course in the Sakura Park. These balloons were made using a biodegradable plastic that can be recycled back into the soil. The air inside the balloons was warmed so the balloons would gradually rise into the air creating an unusual backdrop for the golf course and the town itself. The project was carried out as a workshop in which children from the local community came together to participate.

Design & construction: Ryumei Fujiki + Fujiki Studio, KOU::ARC
Design team: Ryumei Fujiki, Ryoji Ata, Norikazu Ishida, Kosuke Kutsukake, Takaaki Shinohara, Hirotaka Suzuki, Tomonori Tamura, Mamiko Ishizaki, Tomoki Iwashita, Minato Aruga, Yuki Nakamura, Gakuyo Fujimoto, Tsuyoshi Yamagata, Hiroyuki Omori, Shinsuke Kinoshita, Masahiko Sato, Satoshi Shimizu, Yoshio Shimoda, Tatsuya Terashima, Shinya Horikawa, Ikuno Masuda, Yukiko Sato
Client: Art Universiade 2002 Executive Committee
General Director: Fram Kitagawa
Photographs: Eiji Kitada, Ryumei Fujiki

© Ryumei Fujiki

Visitors to the Sakura Park can be seen by those playing on the golf course, thus creating a link that goes in both directions: to and from the course/community. The throng of sunflowers, that inherently ought not to be there, gently sway in the breeze on the pond and are reflected on the water's surface. This unusual scene based on natural elements would doubtlessly be remembered by visitors to the golf course and local residents alike.

© Ryumei Fujiki

© Ryumei Fujiki

© Ryumei Fujiki

© Ryumei Fujiki

The unusual lighting of the floating flowers during the music concert was created by biodegradable plastic, semi-transparent cylinders and light-emitting diodes, which were installed in the center of the Styrofoam holding the sunflowers. They swayed back and forth as if they were dancing, due to the buoyancy of the helium gas injected inside and the force of the wind. Although the event lasted for just a few hours, the combination of music and light produced an effect that was both effective and harmonious.

© Ryumei Fujiki

© Ryumei Fujiki

© Ryumei Fujiki

© Ryumei Fujiki

© Ryumei Fujiki

New Urban Face

Milan, Italy

An initiative set up by the provincial and municipal councils of Milan has converted a tourist information office (IAT) into an "urban parlor" that can host social and cultural events. The "NEWurbanFACE" initiative, designed by Italian architect and designer Simone Micheli, is the product of a commitment to give a different and modern flavor to promotion and communications in the city and its surrounding territory. The venue encourages the exchange and channeling of ideas and information connected with characteristics that make Milan so popular among tourists, i.e. design, fashion and culture. The main purpose is to donate the space to the city, which includes the 4 million citizens who live there and the 10 million or so visitors who visit each year. The project was supported by Antonio Oliverio (Councilor for General Affairs, Tourism and Fashion of the Province of Milan) and Massimiliano Orsatti (Councilor for Tourism, Territorial marketing and Identity of the Municipality of Milan).

The IAT is situated in the Piazza Duomo in an underground section of the former hotel, Albergo Diurno, designed and built by Italian engineer, Cobianchi. One part of the new construction maintains the old style and continues to serve as an information desk for the public, while the modern section becomes a new icon for the city. Information comes in paper format as well as displayed on the 12 monitors and through audio guides that can be downloaded onto mobile phones via Blue Tooth.

When entering the Milan Tourist Point the visitor's attention is drawn by the grace of the variable geometry and by the variety of images. An enormous, green frame acts both as a catering counter and as a reception desk welcoming visitors to the space and giving them a taste of what's to come. The ITA features few but highly effective details: a wide silvery floor spreads through the snow-white curvilinear floor layout, smooth white columns resembling totem poles combine with the textile ceiling lamps with illuminating color-changing bodies, wide and fancy walls are covered by silk screened mirrors with wide video screens and glass and iron flooring allows glimpses of the Roman remains beneath. The yellow skay seats, together with custom-designed mobile furniture and several circular mirrors dispersed over the assembly hall complete the overall picture of the place.

Design: Simone Micheli
Promoters: Antonio Oliverio: Councillor for General Affairs, Tourism and Fashion of the Province of Milan Massimiliano Orsatti: Councillor for Tourism, Territorial marketing and Identity of the Municipality of Milan
Photographs: Jürgen Eheim

The Tubaloon

Kongsberg, Norway

The Tubaloon is a membrane structure designed by the Norwegian architecture firm Snøhetta to serve as the main stage at Scandinavia's reputable Kongsberg Jazz Festival. The annual musical event is one of the oldest and most highly regarded festivals of its kind in Europe and highlights cutting-edge acts from the international jazz world. Mounting of Tubaloon will recur annually for the three-week festival and then be stored in standard containers for the rest of the year. The pneumatic tension membrane structure measures 20 m (65 ft) in height and approximately 40 m (130 ft) in length and seems poised to break away from the tethers which hold it fast to its historic site and drift skyward. Its geometry is suggestive of natural acoustic forms such as musical wind instruments and geometries of the inner ear.

The design brief called for a construction that was easy to erect and that could withstand the abuse of repeated deployment. White Ferrari PVDF coated PVC fabric was chosen for its durability and responsiveness to effects from lighting. The structure type is hybrid, combining 1m (3 ft) diameter pneumatic perimeter tubes with an hour-glass-shaped tension membrane. The decision to support the membrane with a skeleton of 400 mm (16 in) diameter curved galvanized steel tubing was driven by handling logistics: the 5 m (16 ft) long tube sections being the ideal module for container storage, transport and rapid assembly. All foundation points are concealed by discrete utility covers when the Tubaloon is not standing.

Acoustically, the Tubaloon is a dynamic and tunable venue. The form provides a classic clamshell-like shaping over the audience to keep quiet performances intimate while the PVC fabric construction is nearly transparent to sound during amplified performances. The low profile to amplification means that the performances can be controlled simply through the sound mix. An element of chance is introduced by the horn-like opening above the stage. Its orations are encouraged to exit unpredictably out into the surrounding townscape.

Design: Snøhetta AS
Architect: Joshua Teas
Interior architect: Heidi Pettersvold
Landscape architect: Jenny Osuldsen
Structural engineer: Airlight SA
Membrane patterning: FormTL, Radolfzell
Manufacturer: Canobbio SPA
Client: Kongsberg Jazzscener AS
Photographs: Jan Erik Langnes, Robert Sannes

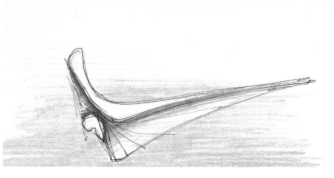

The combination of pneumatics with a tension membrane structure has afforded the Tubaloon a uniquely unified structure. Typical tension membrane systems have external support frames. By contrast, the Tubaloon structure is internalized. The skeleton is dependent on both the pneumatics and the membrane for support in much the same way that the bones of our body are dependent on tendons and skin for their stability. The hybrid structure results in a form that is more voluminous and shapely and it gives the impression that the Tubaloon is a complete biological organism rather than just a skin.

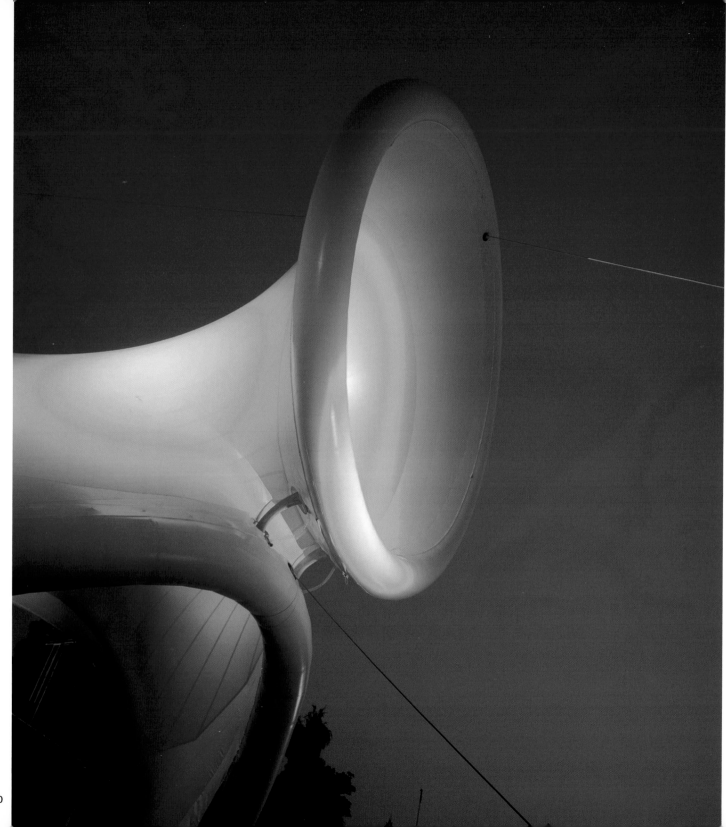

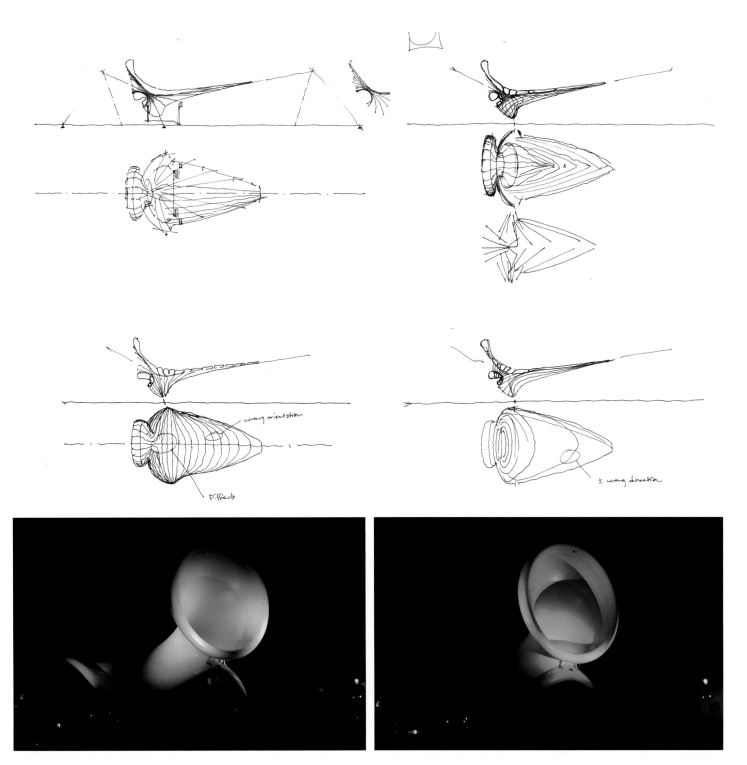

wrong orientation

Difficult

± wrong direction

Enzimi

Rome, Italy

Enzimi is a 10-day festival that takes place every year in different neighbor-hoods of the Italian capital. The event, which is free of charge, comprises two stages for music, a spoken-word theatre and a dance theatre, cinema, meeting space, show spaces, urban projects and a micro-city providing services, information and entertainment. The festival has become known for its cutting-edge structures such as the air terminal used for the Football World Cup and the warehouses of Rome's second largest train station, Ti-burtina, where Lou Reed played in 1998.

For the eighth edition of Enzimi, the festival organizers commissioned Ita-lian architecture studio, Archea Associati, to design and build an exhibition space that would convey the concept of the event through a series of phy-sical structures. The exhibition design consisted of a stage machine con-taining the various informative and functional elements for the different venues included in the programs of dance, entertainment, music, play and café activities.

A landscape of translucent elements was consolidated along an itinerary overlooking the square. The volumes all developed from a standard cube and grew and expanded in all directions, like lighthouses or lenses loo-king towards the city. The constructions followed the Cartesian axes of a free spatial grid, challenging gravity and the vertical design of traditional buildings. Projections and surfaces turned back on themselves, growing and developing to form organic spaces and overhangs that created semi-enclosed outdoor spaces. The translucency of the polycarbonate surfaces projected shadows of the people inside and thus enticed those outside to enter and discover what the space contains.

The graphic design used throughout consisted principally of simple red let-ters, each one occupying a side of a cube, which were spread across the space and together spelled out Enzimi. Each letter represented a different functio-nal area such as a bar, restaurant or Internet point. The graphics created order and united the messages and information associated with the event.

The whole construction rested on a newly built raised metal pavement, on which a host of entertainment activities, a restaurant, a multimedia library and a café were installed. The metal walkway opened up to form a series of squares and meeting points throughout the installation.

Design: Studio Archea
Client: Zone Attive – Comune di Roma
Contractor: Nolostand
Surface area: 1,600 sqm (17,200 sqft)
Photographs: Alessandro Ciampi

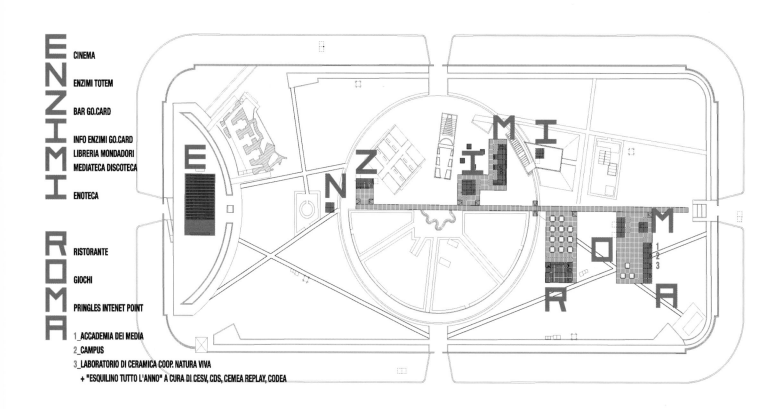

ENZIMI
CINEMA

ENZIMI TOTEM

BAR GO.CARD

INFO ENZIMI GO.CARD
LIBRERIA MONDADORI
MEDIATECA DISCOTECA

ENOTECA

ROMA
RISTORANTE

GIOCHI

PRINGLES INTENET POINT

1_ACCADEMIA DEI MEDIA

2_CAMPUS

3_LABORATORIO DI CERAMICA COOP. NATURA VIVA

+ "ESQUILINO TUTTO L'ANNO" A CURA DI CESV, CDS, CEMEA REPLAY, CODEA

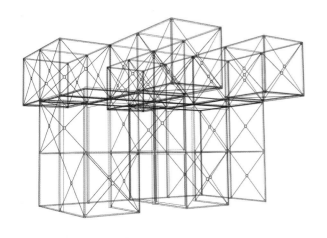

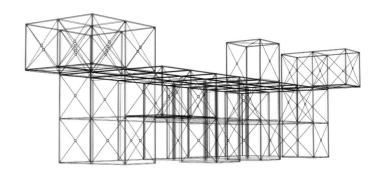

Amstel "The World's Biggest Living Room"

Manchester, United Kingdom

The heart of every football fan in Manchester was on-hand for the UEFA Champions League Final. Amstel built the perfect place for 60 000 fans to prepare for match night, while millions watched from homes and venues across Europe.

The Marketing Objective was to convey the true Amstel experience in a unique locale, inspiring camaraderie of sharing football and beer, using the event to communicate Amstel's core values: Friendship, Fun and Freedom. To appeal to football fans during the UEFA Champions League final, *kubik* inc. fabricated the ultimate, giant living room. It had to be compact enough for storage or transport, yet gigantic and rock-steady when fully constructed, easy to erect and disassemble, as it would be re-used at various events throughout the world. It had to meet demanding safety standards.

The world's biggest living room for Europe's biggest football fans, featured the ultimate chill-out couch (18 × 8 m), a lamp (9 m) and a rug (20 × 18 m). All the oversized furniture was positioned for optimum viewing of the mammoth television screen (8 × 4 m). TBWA agency conceived the idea; *kubik* inc. fulfilled the dream with giant inflatable materials. Thousands of Amstel beer and football fans gained a memorable experience – at home!

During the event, fans from the two finalist teams mingled without a problem, packing the living room throughout the day. They enjoyed the leading product, which significantly incremented sales.

The Living Room attracted, securing worldwide television coverage for the Amstel Giant Living Room, as well as numerous press articles. In the UK, Italy and Holland alone, the media coverage amounted to 29 articles, 12 fully dedicated to Amstel, and 5 Cover Stories. 6 TV specials in the UK; 15 TV specials in Italy; A BBC radio interview. About 40 articles on the internet, with announcements, artist impressions, and photos of fans enjoying the Amstel, Giant Living Room.

Design: *kubik* inc.
Client: Amstel Beer, Heineken International.
Event: UEFA Champions League Finals, 2003
Photographs: contributed by *kubik* inc.

BMW X3 launch and winter driving Xperience

Harbin, China

In order to launch the new BMW X3 on the market in accordance with its new technical features (a new all-wheel drive system called xDrive) an integrated marketing campaign was to be initiated for the first time, which included the first winter driving training in the history of BMW China. In doing so, dealers and journalists were trained to drive the BMW 325i and at the same time shown the BMW X3 LCI "in action" in a winter environment. It also served to establish a high-quality platform for finance and sales conferences.

With the motto "Xperience Xdrive Xtreme", eleven events over seven days accompanied the launch of the BMW X3 in Harbin (China) and the BMW winter training on the frozen Erlong Lake. As part of the integrated event program, participants were presented with the new BMW X3 in an ice house specially constructed for the event, which was heated up to minus five degrees (the outside temperature was minus 20 degrees). The guests were also given the opportunity to place themselves behind the steering wheel on an amazing test drive on road and on the ice of the frozen Erlong Lake, and thus explore the technical features of the new car.

Safety was given top priority. Thus a security inspector was employed by the agency, who guaranteed safety along the entire test track and monitored the stability of the ice house. In order to further emphasize the ice theme, a high-contrast fire and ice concept was developed which acted as a leitmotif throughout the entire program: from the ice house to the general program with fire artistry through to catering in the form of hot and cold food and drinks. Since good weather was one of the basic requirements for the success of the project, the agency even called for a Chinese ceremony for good weather on the frozen Erlong Lake.

Within just 2 months Uniplan designed and implemented an integrated and extensive event program and thus contributed to the successful market launch of the BMW X3 LCI. Over 300 participants, including dealers, journalists, partners and BMW management, took place in the event. Its smooth organization produced seamless transitions from one item on the program to the next. Over the last three days a congress also took place which was orientated primarily towards BMW dealers and partners. This successfully acted as the starting point for the following series of congresses which will take place regularly at BMW China.

Design: Uniplan
Client: BMW China
Photographs: Hans-Georg Esch, Hennef/Sieg, Germany

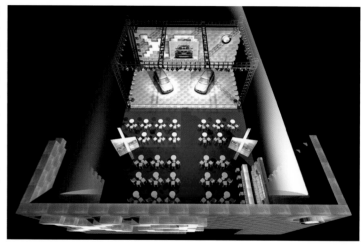

新 BMW X3发布会晚宴
The New BMW X3 Launch Dinner

New 7 Wonders

Lisbon, Portugal

"Our Heritage is our Future" is the motto chosen by the New7Wonders Foundation, under which the group intends to undertake documentation and conservation works of monuments worldwide. This event was set up to announce the seven finalists of an international poll to determine what today's official new seven wonders should be. The event was broadcast live all over the world and took place in Portugal's national Estádio da Luz (Stadium of Light).

Following an opening dance act, acrobats and dancers emerged dramatically from the floor of the stage standing on an enormous stylized globe. The structure rose into the air while the performers danced and flew about suspended from the globe itself and the ceiling of the venue. This was followed by performances from world famous singers including, Jennifer Lopez, Jose Carreras, Dulce Pontes, Chaka Khan, Alessandro Safina and Joaquin Cortez. The event proceeded with the official declaration of the New7Wonders. An enormous book on stage opened up to show the original ancient wonders, which were projected onto the pages, while dancers performed traditional dances. Next followed the presentation of the candidates to the N7W, which was carried out on a gigantic laptop on an LED screen. Appropriately modern dance acts accompanied the announcements. The presentation of the finalists followed, and each representative of the elected wonders was presented with an award in the form of a laptop. Well-known public figures like Neil Armstrong and Cristiano Ronaldo were chosen to present the awards. The event was concluded in spectacular style with an impressive fireworks display.

The event used 1,700 sqm (18,300 sqft) of LED screens which surrounded the entire stage and composed the giant laptop screen. The stage measured a massive 6,000 sqm (64,500 sqft), which gave it a position in the Guinness Book of Records as the biggest stage in history. 360° public visibility allowed all 50,000 spectators to see the action, which was aided by the various under-stage lifts and mechanics. The stage was connected to the VIP stand by a staircase shaped into a giant 7.

Design: Realizar
Direction creation and production: Paulo Sousa Pereira
Live Event Director: Manuel Vaz
Executive Production: Ana Fernandes
Production Manager: Paula Bessone
Production Supervisor: Joao Morais
Production Assistants: Claudia Pimentel, Patricia Vaz and Filipa Oliveira
Event Designer and Build up Coordinator: Luis Sousa Lopes
Volunteers Director: Sérgio Vieira
TV Direction: Manuel Amaro da Costa
TV Producer: Luis Pinto Enes
Talent Director: Carlos Santos
Talent Executive: Simone Sheffield
Stage Manager: Steve Burgess
Scene director: Pedro Lino
Choreography: Jacques Lemay
Choreography assistant: José Mascarenhas
Multimedia Director: José Ramon-Giner
Special effects and pyrotechnics: Joaquim Melo
Sound design: Mike C
Light Designer: Jacinto Alonso
Sound engineer: Rui Soares
Leds and Laser: Telmo Ribeiro
Venue Manager: Copy (Ana Melo)
Logistics: Tiago Montenegro and Daniel Monteiro
Public relations coordinator: Tânia Cunha
Security coordiantion: Américo Martins and Paulo Silva
Media Office: Cláudia Lopes
Photographs: contributed by Realizar

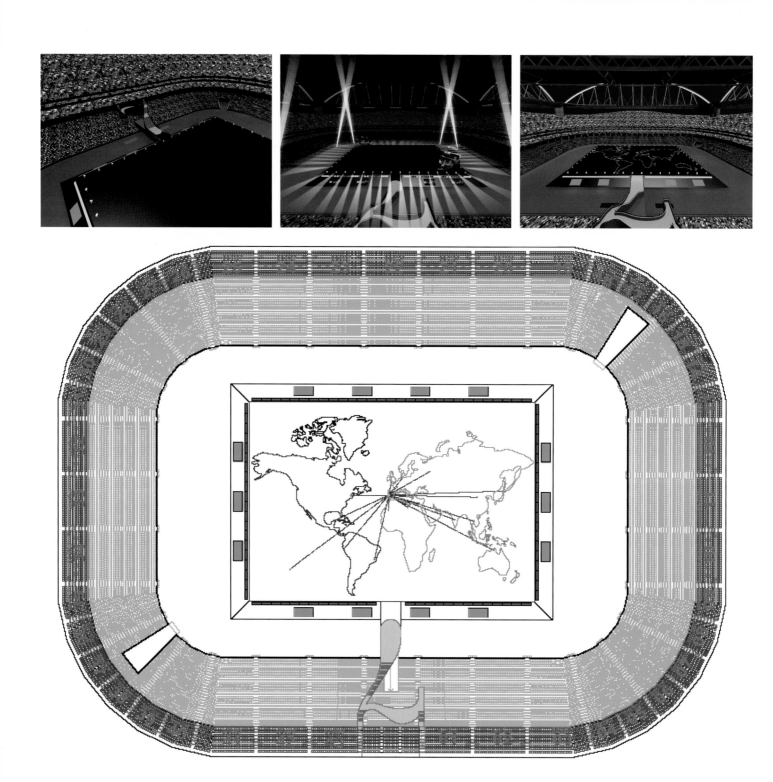

Exhibition, dinner, award presentation and party – NIT LAUS 2006

Barcelona, Spain

Nit Laus is an exhibition and graphic design, advertising and audiovisual award presentation organized annually by the ADG FAD association. However Nit Laus is also a dinner and a party, and one of the few opportunities that professionals have to compete and share experiences in a party atmosphere. The commission for the project clearly defined the different programs: the exhibition of the Laus award finalists (100), dinner for 500 people, award presentation and party.

Each year a venue is chosen along with a different team of event designers that set the character of this competition. In 2006 the Mercat de les Flors was chosen to hold the event, the BOPBAA team for the stage design and the BOOLAB team for the audiovisuals.

The Mercat de les Flors has been witness to many companies who have interpreted its capabilities by transgressing the traditional seating plan and the stage, turning the entire theatre into a single space where actors and public share part of the stage performance. The space contains a semi-extendable tiered seating, a well-equipped technical ceiling that occupies half the room and storage in the basement full of stage design material. The aim of the project was to make the most of all the material and infrastructures the theatre had to offer, using elements, but also the technical staff that usually work in the theater.

The first project decision was to invert the natural position of the stage, transforming the tiers into the award presentation and audiovisual space. This meant that the public was situated where the stage was originally, looking towards the seating, beneath all the theatre's stage machinery, making them the evening's true actors.

The second decision, in tune with the Mercat and with some of the best shows this theatre has seen, was that of leaving the theatre floor free and bringing all the necessary material down from the ceiling, making this the main infrastructure throughout the event. This allowed the space to be transformed by the resources belonging to the theatre and also resolved the logistical problems arising from the dinner, thus avoiding excessive movement of material and people around the room.

Design: BOPBAA Arquitectura
(Josep Bohigas, Francesc Pla, Iñaki Baquero)
Client: ADG FAD
Collaborators: Laura López Fuentes, François Bouju
Audiovisuals: BOOLAB
Graphic Design: Dani Navarro
Construction: La Central de Projectes, Mercat de les Flors technicians
Photographs: Xavi Padrós, Eva Serrats

© Eva Serrats

© Eva Serrats

© Xavi Padrós

24 corrugated, triple layer cardboard tables were suspended from the ceiling complete with cutlery, plates, glasses, food, drink, etc. ready to be lowered and eaten from. From below no one could see them... On entering the room, the tables were at half-height, generating, with the triangular shapes formed from the legs, an illuminated false ceiling, which acted as support to the exhibition of the finalists' graphic work. People entered and visited the exhibition drinking their aperitifs, until the audiovisual began when the alarm sounded for the landing of the tables. A minute later, the 500 people were sitting around the tables with the food laid out and glasses of wine in hands. An instant dinner that avoided waiters having to move around the tables and, like a stage curtain, marked the start of the event.

During the proceeding hour, dinner was eaten and the awards were presented, before the tables rose again (this time above everything) leaving the space free for the party.

© Xavi Padrós

© Xavi Padrós

© Eva Serrats

© Xavi Padrós

© Xavi Padrós

© Xavi Padrós

"Acueducto", Expo Zaragoza 2008

Zaragoza, Spain

This is the winning project of a competition held by Expo Zaragoza 2008 for the construction of an itinerant, ephemeral installation to promote the International Expo in different cities before the event took place. The idea was to define a demountable stage, constructed from shipping containers, which could house exhibitions, meeting spaces and shows, thereby promoting and informing about the Expo. This is why the final shape of the construction is in itself a significant promotional feature. The shape evokes a stretch of an aqueduct, and is constructed in dimensions that would suggest this.

The idea of transit is reinforced by the choice of the recycled shipping containers as a constructive base. While the aqueduct suggests the transportation of water, the containers allude to water as a means of transport. The containers can also be effectively manipulated, are easily adaptable to exhibition uses and, most importantly, suggest the idea of ephemeral architecture.

The construction occupies an area of 20 × 11 m (65 × 36 ft) although the effective space covers more. The image of the stage is that of a single unit, although it is constructed from a combination of 13 containers of different sizes: 0.90, 1.80 and 3.60 m (3, 6 and 11 ft). The final volume creates a long, narrow and high façade with rectangular spaces behind that act as buttresses. The ensemble can be divided into three areas: the arch, which can be used as a stage, the interior exhibition space and the exterior area, with an information point and space for programmed events.

The arch is formed from three columns made from three levels of containers piled on top of each other like a lintel. The base of one of the columns is used as the information point; it is the only container that has been manipulated to be structurally reinforced and made more accessible for maintenance.

Design: BOPBAA Arquitectura
Client: Expo Zaragoza 2008
Associates: François Bouju, Soledad Armada and Sara Atsuara
Structure: Carles Campanyà
Developer: Corporactiva S.L. and Edelman Spain S.A. (Joaquim Bech de Careda and Perxàs)
Installations: César Raso García
Lighting: ARTEC
Photographs: Xavier Padrós

The space for events is formed by the protection that the positioning of the containers offers and by the presence of a large awning. The space can be adapted for meetings, projections and gastronomic demonstrations. It has a capacity of 70 people, although its limits are not defined by a rigid enclosure. There are two natural access points that can be closed off with ephemeral, moveable elements. The longest container is partially open showing a lineal sofa that acts as a theater box for viewing the events.

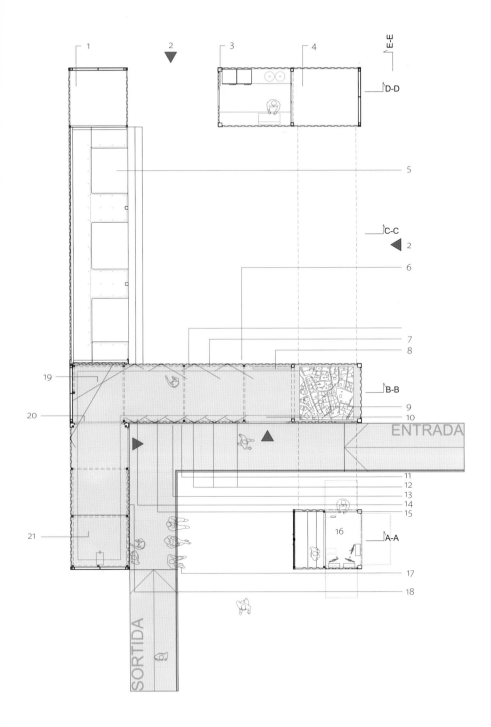

ENTRADA

SORTIDA

E-E

D-D

C-C

B-B

A-A

1 2 3 4

5

6

7
8

9
10

11
12
13
14
15

16

17

18

19

20

21

The exhibition is considered as a linear circuit that begins at the information point. A ramp organizes the queues and balances out the changing level between the public spaces and the horizontal line of the base of the containers. Those that house the exhibition form an L that protects the exterior exhibition. The access to this space is through an opening in the side. Inside the containers unfold through four different display systems: luminescent methacrylate posters, interactive photography, models and overhead projections. One visit is expected to last between 5 and 15 minutes and has a capacity for no more than 20 people at any one time.

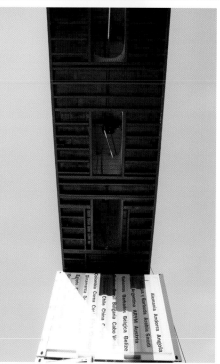

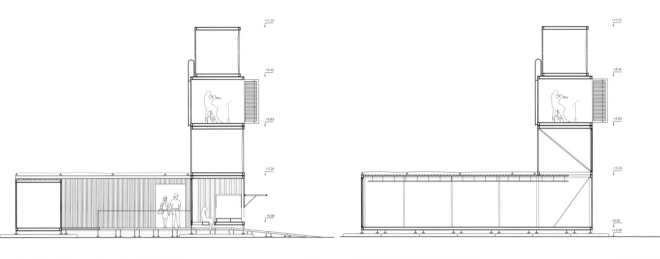

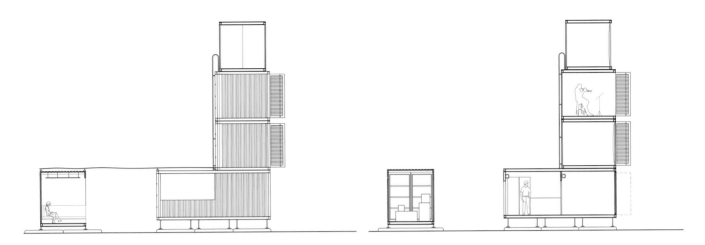

50 Years of DIT

Frankfurt, Germany

The Alte Oper, a major concert hall in Frankfurt, Germany, was chosen to host the 50-year anniversary of the renowned international fund manager, dit–Allianz Global Investors. This famous venue was to acquire a futurist-oriented environment for the event, which as well as honoring the company's tradition and its half-century long success record, also had to highlight the company's ability to adjust towards the future and its innovative power. The integration of a modern aesthetic into a famous, historic building produced the ideal combination of the traditional with the contemporary.

Under the motto "Change.Growth.Future" an architectural production placed the guests in the center of the event. Starting from the stage, large media-played ribbons created a three-dimensional sculpture that stretched to the back of the hall, wrapping around the audience. This eliminated the distance to the stage thus converting the guest into one of the actors in the event. The installation allowed the stage setting to unfold throughout the hall. The highlighted media ribbon, with its smooth transitions and whose rising format was associated with the curve of rising share prices, deliberately played with the optical perception and dissolved accepted visual patterns, generating curiosity and attracting attention.

A lively and communicative atmosphere developed in the hall. During the artistic and cinematic interpretations of the themes and the history of dit, a great variety of sequences developed, which, through the dynamic geometry of the projection screens, took the guests on a holistic journey through time.

Concept and design: Dreizueins (Boris Banozic)
Client: dit - Allianz Dresdner Global Investors
Project manager: Ralph Scheurer, Quasar Communication
Construction: Swen Neubauer, Ewenture
Media: Group-IE, Coolux, Fischer&Friends
Photographs: Jürgen Zeller, transform-mag

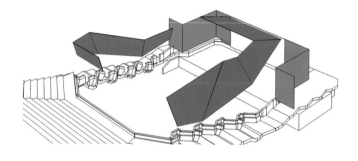

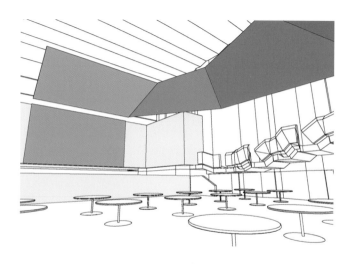

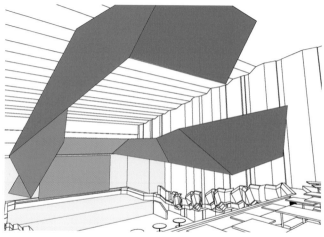

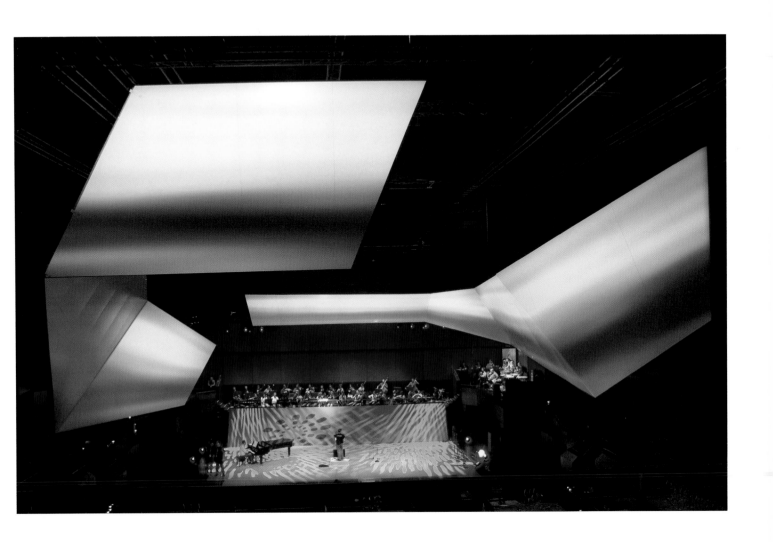

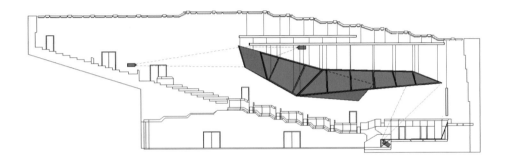

Nike Football Park 2002

various countries

13 parks in 13 countries in 4 continents: Nike's vision was to celebrate soccer – the athletes and the fans – by building awesome, interactive Sports Parks. To move away from "mainstream" marketing they felt they could establish loyalty and respect with their youth target market by creating a raw, "street", underground feel.

Nike wanted their involvement with soccer to go beyond technical merit, into the importance of being a team. The significance of their Scorpion logo lies in the message "Every touch counts"; it's not important how fast you run, but that each movement contributes to your team's goal. This vision would tie into Nike's Legacy plan – to keep their marketing message alive by leaving something behind.

Nike hoped to reach 1.2 million kids during the 30-day period.

kubik inc. (formerly Exhibits International) worked closely with Nike on the entire image, from the cage used in the television commercial, to helping Nike choose the most appropriate sites. They created incredible parks out of an abandoned abattoir, an unfinished subway line and an old ship to recreate parts of the television commercial.

Each Park contained indoor and outdoor interactive areas. The edge Nike desired was created through aged metal walls, cages around the interactive games areas, stacked oil drums and sea containers, spray painted logos and team posters plastering the walls. Each indoor venue housed the infamous "Scorpion Cage" that mirrored the television commercials and held the intense 3-minute final team matches. A central cage with a DJ added a "rave" feeling in the indoor section of each Park while video presentations and an animated scorpion played across large monitors.

The team of designers, technicians, builders and installers worked in 10 languages. The latest lighting and sound technology was used. This logistically challenging project saw all 13 Parks launched on schedule and was a resounding success, exceeding Nike's attendance objective by thrilling 1.8 million kids.

Some countries have kept the Parks open as sports parks for public use. As many of these parks were built in run down areas, they are a satisfying contribution to Nike's legacy program.

Design: *kubik* inc.
Client: Nike, Inc.
Photographs: Contributed by *kubik* inc.

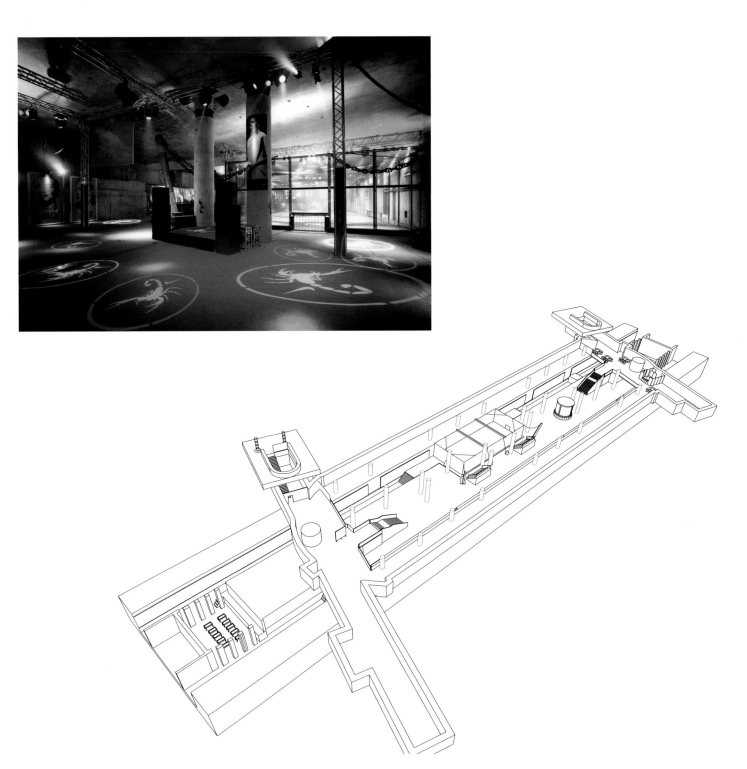

Previous page: The Berlin event
Top: Tokyo
Top left: Madrid
Bottom left: Paris
Next page: Rotterdam

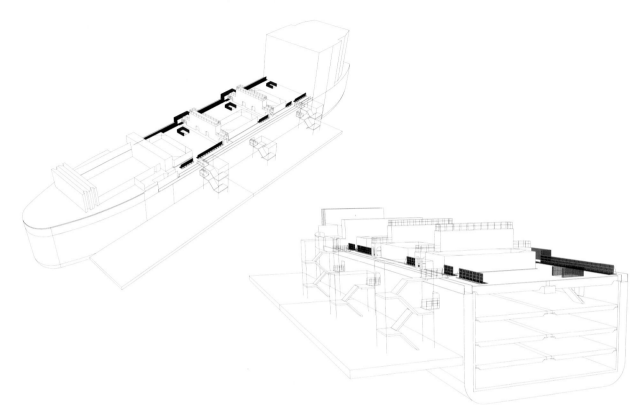

Festivalzentrum Theaterformen

Braunschweig, Germany

Once every two years, for ten days, Braunschweig's Municipal Theater becomes the venue for Theaterformen, the biennial theater festival that has gradually earned itself a respected international reputation. The brief commissioned by the Staatstheater Niedersachsen GmbH involved creating a temporary festival center to provide a meeting point, with program information desks, ticket sales booths, a library, and a small café.

On this occasion these essential facilities have been interpreted by the architects as the pretext to offer the public and the inhabitants of the town an altered vision of the that part of the city, and a new way of experiencing the festival: the theater's ballroom, located in the upstairs rooms of the imposing building, and which is normally reserved for the audience during the intermissions, was converted temporarily into a festival center. For ten days, this introverted space, usually only accessible to theater goers, unknown to many local people, became a freely accessible public area. Independently of theater performances, the center played host to a mixed crowd, drawn in partly by live projections of World Cup soccer matches.

The structural intervention consisted in erecting a broad staircase on a framework of scaffolding that could be assembled and dismantled within two days. This structure fulfilled the function of connecting the square in front of the theater to the balcony of the ballroom. Tall steps for sitting at the center of the south-facing staircase made it a grandstand during the daytime. In a sense, the city became the stage, the theater became the stalls. The view follows the prominent street axis between the theater, which is set at the historical ramparts of the city, and Braunschweig's old city center. During the festival, audiences entered and left the theater directly via the steps. The red carpet used on the staircase and in the ballroom becomes both an invitation and an emblem for the festival, visible from afar. The structure creates a ceremonial and dramatic sign, reminiscent of an Aztec pyramid, that expresses all the mystery that theater has to offer.

Design: Kühn Malvezzi, with Jan Ulmer
Client: Staatstheater Niedersachsen
(Veronica Kaup-Hasler)
Photographs: Ulrich Schwarz, Timm Ringewaldt, Kühn Malvezzi

© Ulrich Schwarz

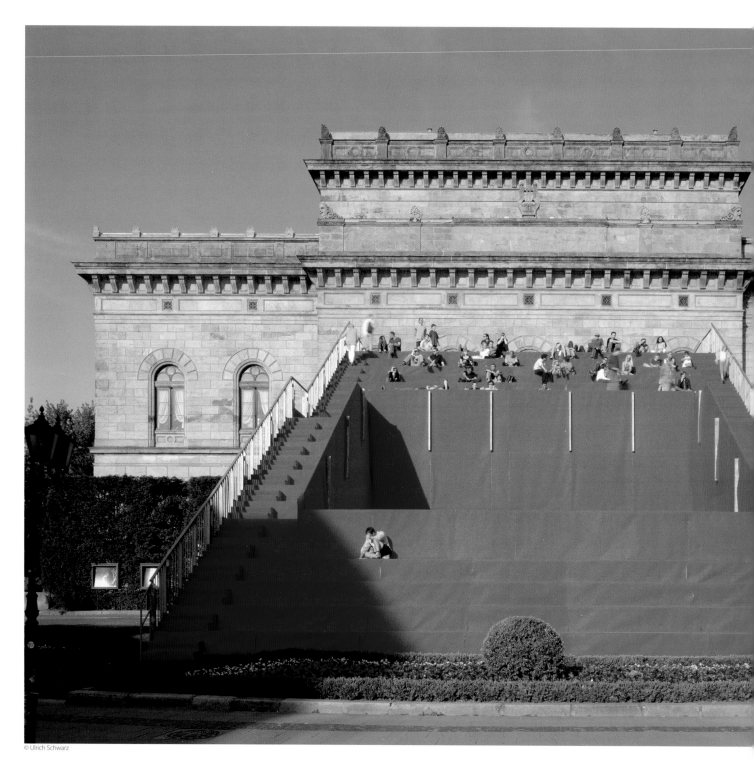

© Timm Ringewaldt

© Kühn Malvezzi

© Timm Ringewaldt

© Kühn Malvezzi

© Kühn Malvezzi

© Timm Ringewaldt

© Kühn Malvezzi

Hugo Boss Yacht Christening

Hamburg, Germany

Inspired by the remarkable atmosphere of Hamburg's Harbor, LIGANOVA staged a lavish event for Hugo Boss to celebrate the official christening of the Hugo Boss sailing yacht. High above the heads of the 1000 VIP and celebrity guests, a giant crane slowly lowered the 300-ton yacht into the dock. This spectacular event was accompanied by a breathtaking lightshow from Berlin light designer Gerd Hof, whilst an exclusively developed sound by DJ Westbam complimented the visual experience. The array of lighting was vast, with a total of five million watts illuminating the Hamburg harbor during the traditional champagne christening ceremony.

Immediately following the service, the old fish auction hall became a party location. The unique industrial atmosphere interplayed with a colossal installation of disco balls, together with driving beats to provide the appropriate after-show mood. Culinary delights such as currywurst with gold leaf as a midnight snack completed the evening

Design: Liganova
Light design: Gerd Hof
Client: Hugo Boss
Photographs: contributed by Liganova

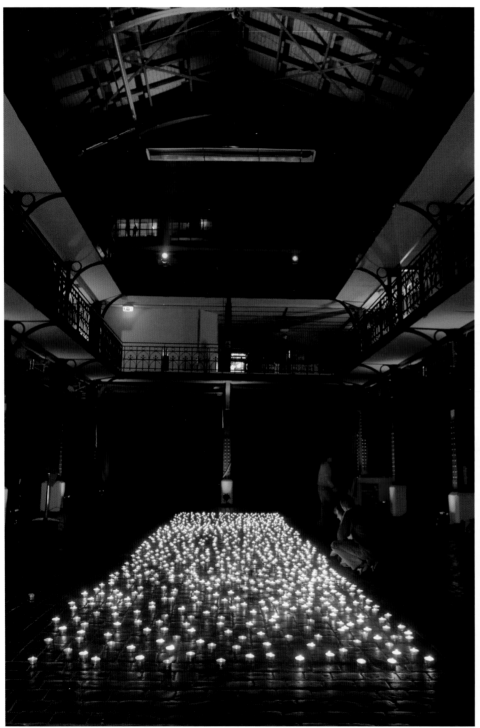

Yard furniture MuseumsQuartier Vienna

Vienna, Austria

This bizarre yet attractive furniture has served as an indispensable feature of the courtyards found in Vienna's MuseumsQuartier, and is known popularly as Enzi furniture. It was designed by the architectural team Popelka Poduschka architekten with the aim of enlivening these spaces and bringing some dynamism to an otherwise static environment.

These unusual pieces of furniture are cut from Styrofoam blocks meaning that although they are large, they are also surprisingly light. This affords them the advantage of being easily changed and rearranged (by forklift), thereby offering an organic space, which evolves and changes with time. They are also repainted each year adding another factor to their evolution. Their variety of colors and shapes brings a touch of cheer to this space, which has been criticized by some for being excessively somber. Although hard, the furniture has proved to be perfectly comfortable, since they have been used by children and the elderly alike. Their solidness also protects them from getting damaged or worn out by use. Furthermore, they are economically more viable than more commonly used outdoor, urban furniture, which in addition to being more expensive is also much more permanent.

The blocks do not necessarily have to be used exclusively as seating. They can be placed on top of each other and joined, with relative ease, to create enclosed spaces, walls, bars, public booths, etc. In fact originally they were used as igloos, where people could go to drink punch in the cold Austrian winter. The end result of these Styrofoam modules is that the courtyards of MuseumsQuartier have developed into one of Vienna's liveliest public spaces.

Design: PPAG Architekten, Anna Popelka, Georg Poduschka
Client: Enzi
Photographs: PPAG, Alex Koller, Studio Krauss, Alexander Kaltenbach, Hermann Czech, Lisi Gradnitzer

© PPAG

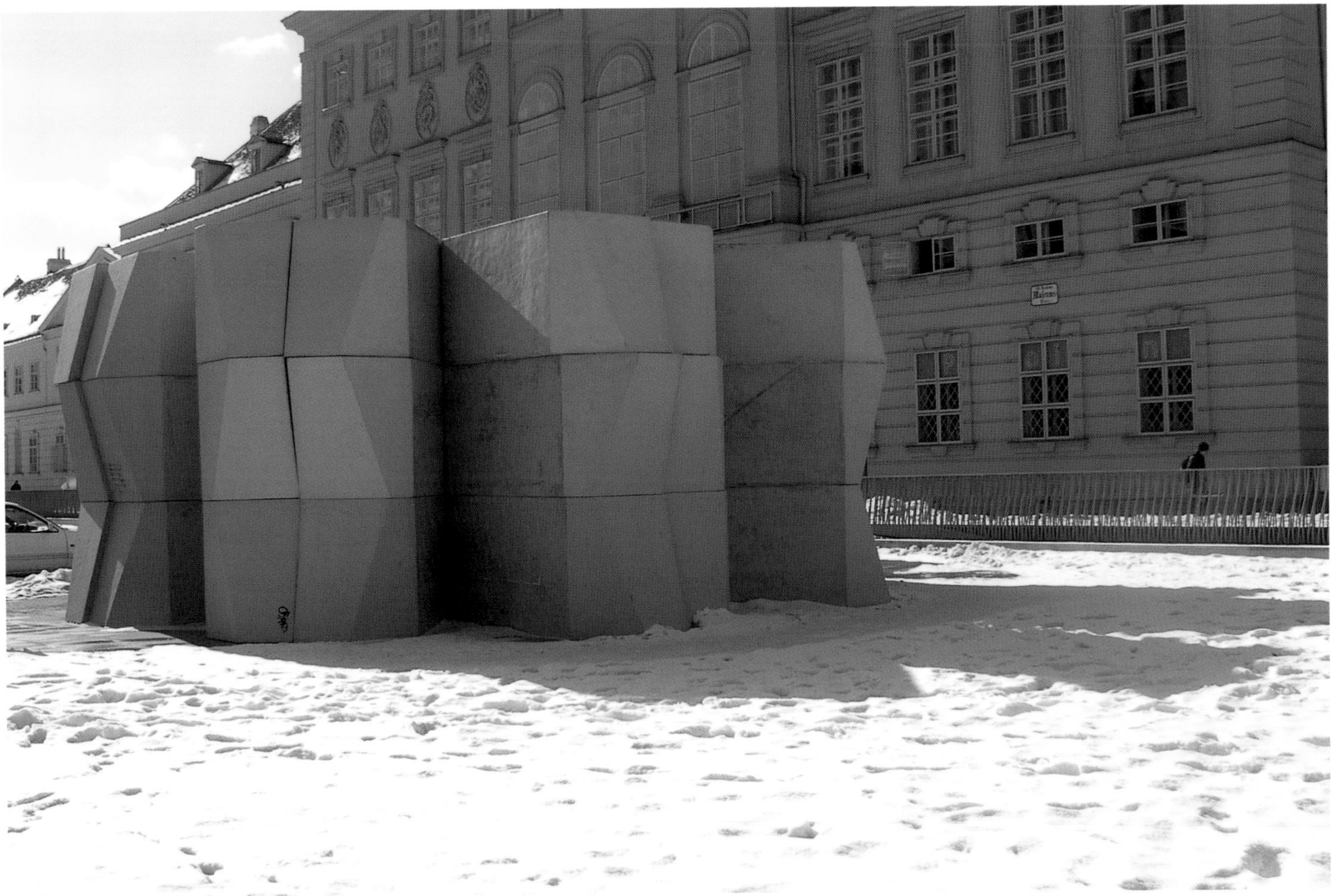

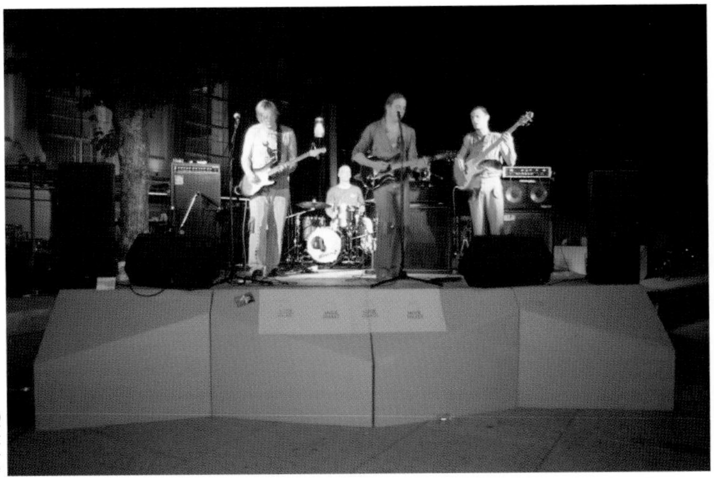

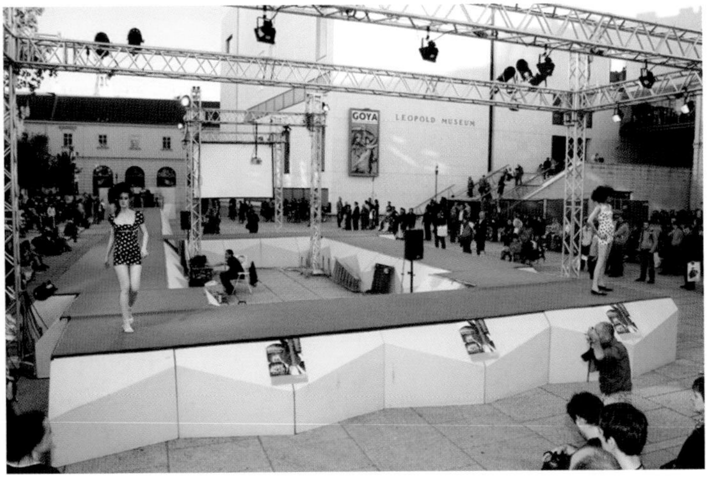
GOYA
LEOPOLD MUSEUM

© Studio Krauss

© PPAG

© PPAG

© PPAG

© PPAG

100 years of Röhm

Darmstadt, Germany

Evonik Röhm is a German-based company that specializes in the manufacture of chemicals and plastics. To commemorate the company's 100th anniversary they commissioned design studio Voss+Fischer to create an installation that would reflect the company's philosophy, their products and their long history. The gala evening was planned to take place in a spacious room located on the company grounds in Weiterstadt, Germany. One of the requirements was that the installation had to integrate products manufactured by Evonik Röhm.

The design concept chosen for the event was that of a contemporary chandelier, an object which is traditional and elegant yet at the same time, in this case, conveyed innovation and flare. Voss+Fischer suspended 100 rectangular Perspex panes of different sizes and colors from the ceiling of the venue, one for each year since the company was founded. The panes were arranged in concentric circles and angled so as to form the enormous chandelier. The lighting shone from the structure highlighting the bold and bright colors of the Perspex. As the lights changed color so did the Perspex, creating an array of eye-catching theatrical effects. Since the installation was the only source of light in the room it captured the attention of everyone present.

This modern take on the traditional chandelier succeeded in transmitting the image of a bold and innovative company, which at the same time is well established and reliable; a balanced combination of bright colors and sturdy geometries.

Design: VOSS+FISCHER
Client: Evonik Röhm GmbH
Photographs: contributed by VOSS+FISCHER

Autostadt

Wolfsburg, Germany

Volkswagen's Autostadt or "Car City" is effectively a car dealership and theme park rolled into one. It allows the company to present its values to the public as well as display its products. It tells the story of VW's past and offers an insight into their technological know-how by way of guided tours through the factory. Autostadt, however, is not just a presentation of the corporation itself. It is an attempt to strengthen the dialogue between the company and its clients, and also promote a dialogue between the city, its inhabitants and Autostadt. The latter is partly why the park presents different events for the public to enjoy.

WES and Partner is a firm of landscape architects who were commissioned by Autostadt to come up with various buildings and installations for the park. The firm developed and monitored several of their temporary events such as "Winterspiele" (Winter Games) and "Frühlingserwachen" (Spring Awakening) which were both held at the park

The Winterspiele saw the park turned into a magical landscape of lights and music. The event included a variety of installations that were related to the season. The most interactive of these was an ice-skating rink, which the public could use during the day and night. In the evenings there were also ice-skating shows accompanied by live music played on a glass stage suspended above the rink. The event included an artificial ski slope and an ice tower.

For the Frühlingserwachen, enormous eggs were distributed randomly across the park, which the public could interact with by touching or even climbing over them. The eggs were decorated with bright colors to enliven the grounds of the park and combine with the sea of yellow daffodils that appears at this time of year.

Design: WES & Partner
Schatz · Betz · Kaschke · Wehberg-Krafft
Landscape Architects
with Max Wehberg
Client: Autostadt GmbH
Photographs: WES & Partner / Jörn Hustedt

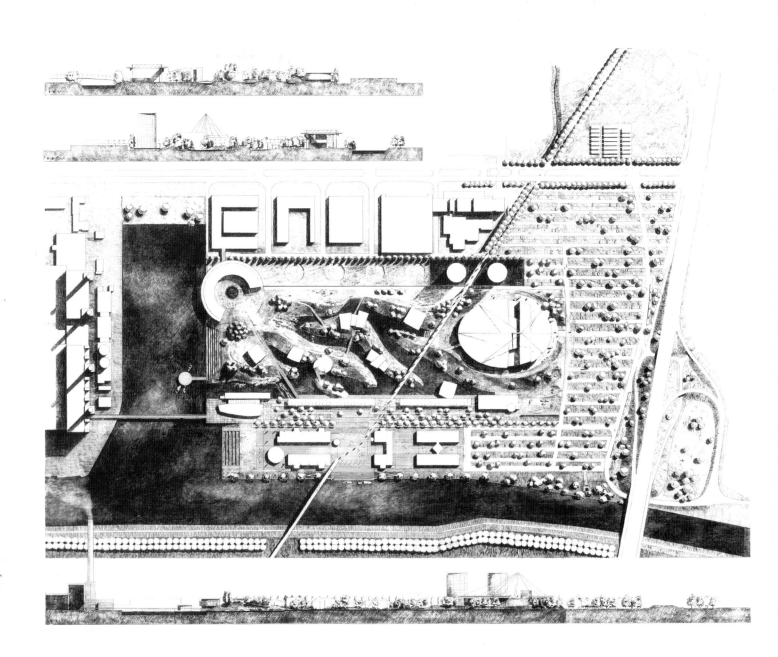

Opposite page: Views of the Winterspiele
This page: The eggs in the Frühlingserwachen

Lilas

London, UK

This installation for the annual Serpentine Summer Party was designed as an open air space that consists of three identical tensile fabric structures or parasols, which rise to a height of 5.5 m (18 ft) and are spread around a central point. Each parasol develops sculpturally from a small articulated base to a large cantilevered diamond shape and is supported by a steel frame, which is covered in a fire resistant fabric. As well as their appealing aesthetics these structures also had a more functional purpose: to protect partygoers from the potentially wet English summer.

Taking inspiration from complex natural geometries such as flower petals and leaves, the three parasols overlap to create the pavilion's main conceptual feature: complex symmetry, interweaving all-the-while without touching, allowing air, light and sound to travel through narrow gaps in a state that is both open and likewise tending toward closure. To ensure that the overall appearance of the parasols was fluid, the fabric was rolled over support rings at the top and bottom of the structures. This overlapping ensures that the fabric forms a continuous line around the tube. All connections are therefore hidden from sight when stood at ground level.

Raised on a low platform located within an open field and flanked by a row of trees just South of the Serpentine Gallery, the Serpentine Summer Party Pavilion is free standing and accessible from all sides. It basically consists of an oblong base made of steel, with a surface area of 315 sqm (3400sqft), which is covered in plywood and then finished with a slip resistant resin. Accommodating movement throughout the site, the Pavilion is enigmatic. During the day it provides shade, while at night the pavilion undergoes an energetic transformation into a source of illumination. From continuous lighting around each base, light is thrown up the fabric surfaces along very thin seams that radiate about the parasols. These act as corseting or the veining of flowers revealing the geometric intricacy of the pavilion and highlighting the overall architectural form in calligraphic arcs.

Design and architecture: Zaha Hadid with Patrik Schumacher
Project architect: Kevin McClellan
Consultants: Structural ARUP
Steel fabrication: Sheetfabs Ltd.
Membrane fabrication: Base Structures Ltd.
Lighting design: Zumbotel
Furniture provided by:
Estabished & Sons
Kenny Schachter
Sawaya & Moroni
Serralunga
Max Protetch
Swarovski
Client: Serpentine Gallery
Photographs: Luke Hayes

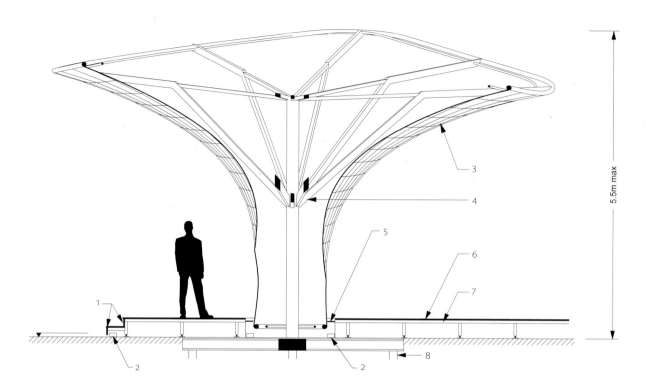

1. Riser to painted black to match flooring with opening at lower edge for lighting
2. Perimeter flourescent step lighting by Zumtobel
3. PVC tensile fabric on steel frame patterned and installed by Base Structures
4. Tube steel column and cantilevered support frame painted with off-white rust retardant primer
5. 6 mm 'opal' plexi site cut to fit fabric profile mounted on brackets
6. 1.2 × 2.4 plywood decking with Ragupol surfacing on steel frame
7. 1.2 × 2.4 tubular steel frame with adjustable legs with rust retardant primer
8. 4.5 m screw pile typ

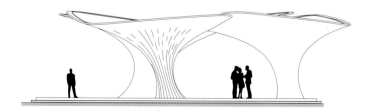

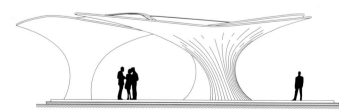

Elle Decor

Milan, Italy

Elle Decor wished to display their latest trends in interior decoration and domestic design by association, with an important focus on the artifacts and furniture designed by Quinze & Milan, who also designed the display itself. The designers had 3 containers placed in one of the city's urban parks, bringing their ideas directly to the attention of the public during what is potentially one of the most contemplative moments of the day, when people are most observant and open to consider new possibilities.

The idea, according to Quinze & Milan, was to create a submerged living cell in the middle of a park. Whatever the case may be, each of the modules was fitted out in a predominant color. Whether, in this case, red, blue or green had anything to do with earth, water and fire, is an interpretation that the designers prefer not to determine any further. Nevertheless, there is something alchemical about their work; the transmutational way in which the expected qualities of everyday utensils are altered, defies the boundaries between furniture and sculpture; soft becomes hard, solid becomes flowing, movable is fixed, rigid becomes flexible.

The containers are decorated by the designers' graphic team Glossy. The exteriors' different colors do not affect the decorative subject matter which shows a classical pseudo-oriental scene of stylized vegetation, exotic birds and butterflies, in the manner of blatantly "retro" upholstery and wallpaper. It is only inside each of the containers that the graphic details establish links with the color, rounded forms for blue, more angular shapes for red....

Each volume houses a minimalistic installation of Quinze & Milan furniture. Natural elements invade the indoor space and interact with the armchairs and tables, tinted fluorescent tubes alter the visitors' perception of the rectangular room, where mass production meets nature in an aesthetically refined illustration of contemporary lifestyles.

Design: Quinze and Milan (Arne Quinze)
Client: Elle Decor
Photographs: contributed by Quinze and Milan

Australian Pavilion

The Pavilion captures the interior atmosphere of the National Swimming Centre for the Beijing 2008 Olympics - 'Watercube' designed by PTW Architects, CSCEC+design and ARUP.

The Watercube's exterior relates to traditional Chinese architecture, an orthogonal counterpoint to the main Olympic stadium's curves, but the interior translates water and bubbles into fluidity and randomness.

Based on the existing 180 x 180 m (590 x 590 ft) bubblebox, the lightweight construction of the new pavilion follows the tension lines of soap films, stretching between ground and sky. Since the early seventies and Frei Otto's soap bubble experiments with the Munich Olympic stadium, naturally evolving systems have gained ground in the field of new building typologies. Not exactly "designed", the pavilion is the most efficient subdivision of three-dimensional space, achieved with a flexible material that follows the forces of gravity, tension and growth, like a spider's web or a coral reef. Atmospheric animations projected onto it bring the pavilion to life as a surreal underwater experience.

The material is a fire rated Nylon Lycra Fabric. The installed object occupies a space of 24 x 10 x 6 m (79 x 33 x 20 ft). Packed for transport, it fits into a large sports bag and weighs 77 pounds. Assembly can be carried out in 1 hour, besides the rigging structure from which it is suspended. It was designed in 4 weeks, from the initial sketch to installation. PTW delivered a 3D computer-model, which Taiyo Membrane Corporation processed with a sailmaking software application to simulate stresses and tensions in the fabric, showing how the shape of membrane would respond. When the buildable design was ready, the 103 pieces of Lycra were stitched together in 200 hours of manual labor. The finished item was packed and transported to Beijing as "hand-luggage". Installed for the first time at the Stadia China exhibition within the budgeted sum, it has since travelled to DESIGNEX in Melbourne and to Dubai.

The project tests a new style of digital workflow, capable of generating a product of any shape out of lightweight material in an extremely short time. Easy to travel with, it can be built in 1 hour, and is fully reusable after the event.

Design: PTW Architects
Client: Australian Pavillion
Photographs: contributed by PTW

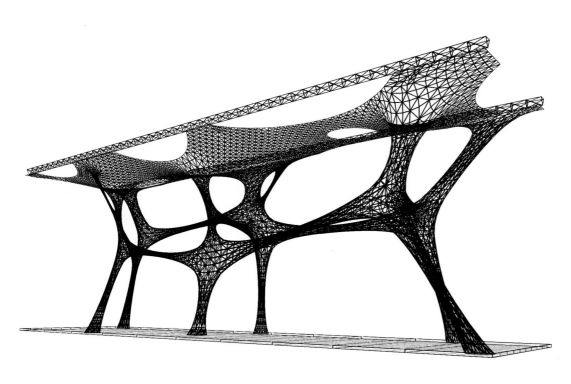

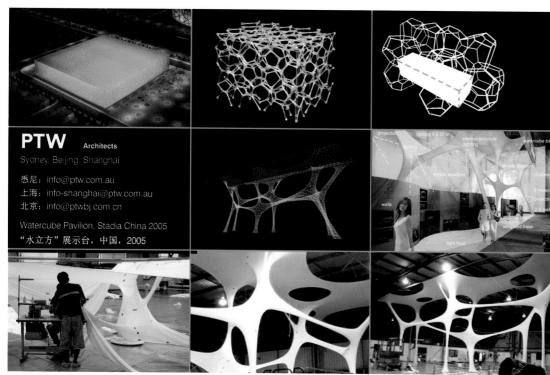

PTW Architects

Sydney, Beijing, Shanghai

悉尼：info@ptw.com.au
上海：info-shanghai@ptw.com.au
北京：info@ptwbj.com.cn

Watercube Pavilion, Stadia China 2005
"水立方" 展示台，中国，2005

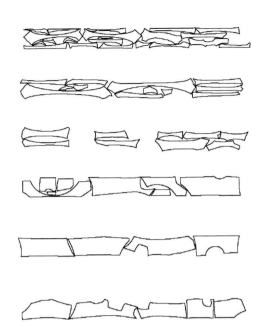

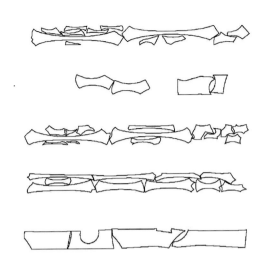

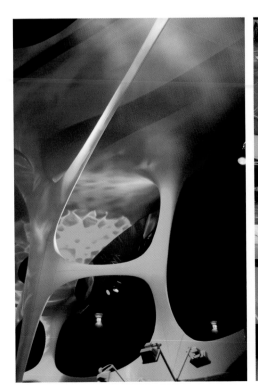

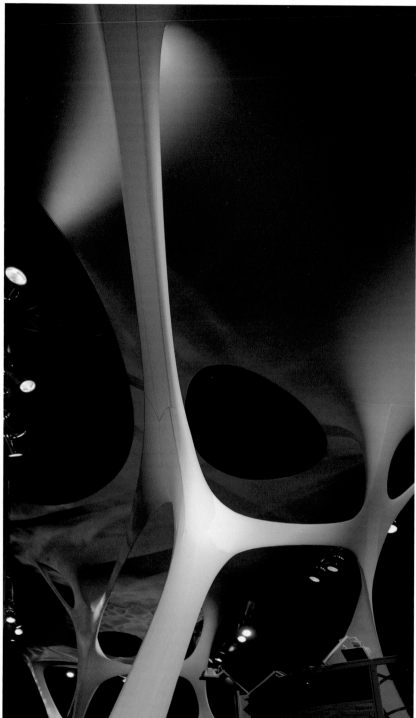

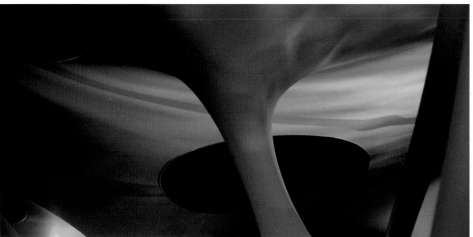
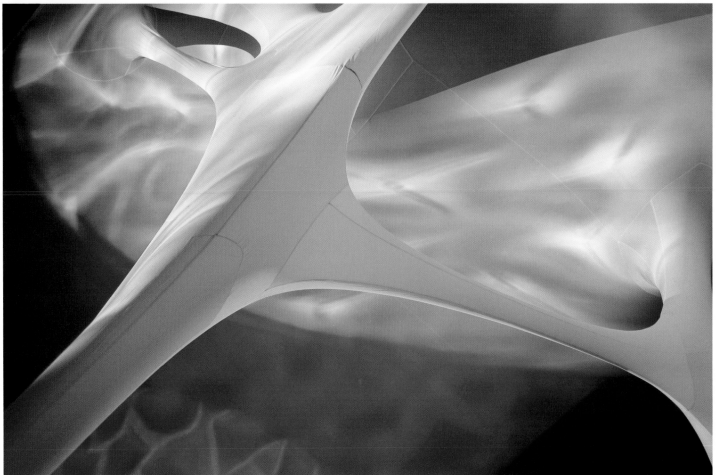

Time Line/The Québec City Carnaval

Quebec, Canada

The Quebec Carnaval wanted to renew the image of its traditional Ice Palace by developing an installation based on the theme of the ice garden. The choice was motivated by the idea of offering the public the possibility of exploring the world of ice through a new theme while creating a very real but transitory public square that would greet approximately 100,000 people over a 14 day period. The location for the installation was the Place de l'Assemblée Nationale, which is bordered by the walls of Quebec City and Saint Louis Street and faces the National Assembly.

The design organized an itinerary with which the public could explore different aspects of the world of ice. The project presented itself as a linear trajectory that transported visitors through time and ordered the sequence of their journey. Double walls led to four overlapping chronological themes for which precise atmospheres and volumes were developed.

The Ice Age was evoked using deliberately oversized sheets of ice, randomly scattered, that appeared to interact like tectonic plaques. This took visitors back 10,000 years to when the nearby Saint Lawrence River Valley was buried under ice. The igloo, symbol of nomadic shelter and the Far North brought visitors back to the snow forts of their youth. It stood 15 m (50 ft) high, and had at its core a pilaster and a frozen pond. Its thick inner walls brought to mind 3,000 years of Inuit construction. Colonization was evoked by an ice village, made up of houses that provided an imaginary glimpse of life in the distant past. It explored a landscape beginning to be structured by man. Finally, small towers of ice evoked the urban towers that adorn the horizon of modern-day Quebec. The ice and snow used throughout highlighted the transitory nature of things. A passageway formed by translucent ice walls led visitors from one space to another, through glistening walls, ordering the journey's sequence and stops. Main entrances to the installations acted as reference points but each thematic space was open to the surrounding urban environment, offering a unique vantage point onto contemporary life, as seen from inside an ephemeral ice universe.

Throughout the day and night, the contact with snow and ice was constantly being modified by natural and artificial lighting, heightening sensory perception and accentuating the site's mysteries. The project became a place for public assembly, providing visitors with a new and renewed reading of their surrounding landscape and territory.

Design: Pierre Thibault
Client: Québec Carnaval
Photographs: Pierre Thibault

Passageways constructed from blocks of ice led visitors from one installation to the next. Each installation however, was open to the urban surroundings offering visitors the chance to see their everyday environment from this ephemeral ice garden.

heaven is a place on earth

Wattens, Austria

This sophisticated veil was designed and built for the Swarovski factory in Wattens, Austria. Visitors treat the factory gate as a threshold to a secret, to the origin of the crystal myth, so with this in mind, Markus Langes-Swarovski and the site office team opened a competition which was won by the German architectural studio d e signstudio regina dahmen-ingenhoven.

The 250 m (820 ft) long veil embraces the factory grounds so that the entire entrance area becomes a "landmark", a synthesis of the arts. It not only veils, but also functions as a gate. The semi-transparent material does not disclose the Swarovski secret. Instead, it allows for the onlooker to surmise it. Even the opposite side of the street is incorporated in the shape of a grove lined with silver limes. This creates a fluid transition to the public space. Veil, landscaping, illumination and the design of the space merge to become a breathtaking backdrop.

The veil is made of a corrosion-and weather-resistant stainless steel mesh. It gives rise to a varied play of light and embodies unique material qualities. The veil is held in place by a 10 m (32 ft) high steel stringer. A group of illuminated pads creates a seating arrangement and doubles as the boundary to what lies beyond. During the day, rays of sun and traveling clouds revel in this space, triggering a constant change. When night falls, a spectacle takes place that lives in harmony with the hues of the sky. This setting forms the groundwork for a permanent and enchanting transformation.

Design: d e signstudio regina dahmen-ingenhoven
Client: Swarovski
Photographs: Holger Knauf / Thomas Schuepping

© Holger Knauf ▶

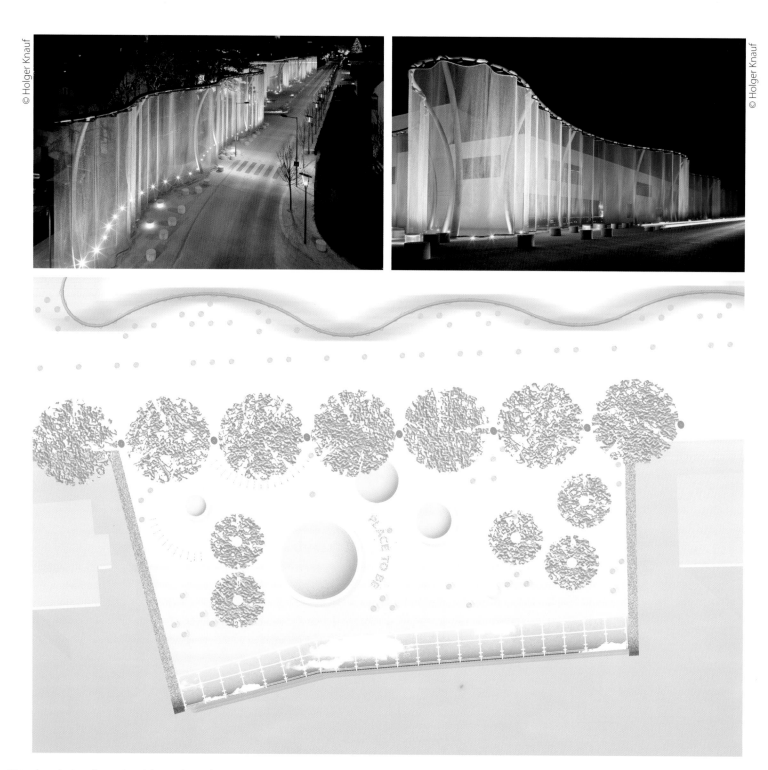

PLACE TO BE

POWER OF UNIT

© Thomas Schuepping

d e signstudio regina dahmen-ingenhoven **287**

Blaue Nacht

Nuremberg, Germany

The Blaue Nacht (Blue Night) takes place each year in Nuremberg, Germany. The summer festival implies an evening full of artistic performances and installations. For just one night all of the city's museums and theatres open their doors and many landmarks are transformed into ephemeral works of art. In 2006 the German artist Rosalie was invited by the festival organizers to create an installation for the event. Rosalie's artistic work is marked by aspects of an innovative transgression of limits, which is clearly present in this piece.

Right in the very heart of this historic city Rosalie set up 150 blue, helium-filled, spherical balloons each measuring between 1.5 m (5 ft) and 2.5 m (8 ft) in diameter, creating an enormous temporary architectural addition to the town center. A complex system of lines was used to keep the balloons in place. Each is connected by around 20 individual strings which meet to form one main line. All these different lines then meet and cross over to form a structurally solid netting, which is anchored to platforms floating in the river below.

The blue balls formed a sharp contrast between their contemporary appearance and the aesthetics of this historic city. Dubbed by the artist as "sky wings" the blue layer appeared as if either a part of the sky had been trapped at the level of the city, or if the Pegnitz River had risen into the air. The installation was set to float just above the level of the riverside paths and next to a bridge so people could see it from inside the town. From this perspective a mysterious line of blue floated on the horizon above the crowds. With this installation Rosalie blurred distinctions between the heavens and earth and between the traditional and the modern. The name "…wherever rest thy gentle wings…" was taken from a poem written by the German poet Fredrich Schiller that expresses how mankind can be saved through acts of solidarity between people. Beethoven later used the poem in his famous piece of music 'Ode to Joy'.

Design: rosalie
Client: NÜRNBERG LEUCHTETE
Photographs: contributed by rosalie

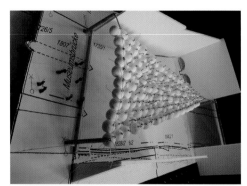
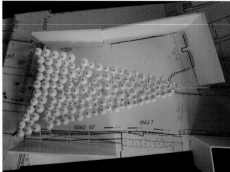
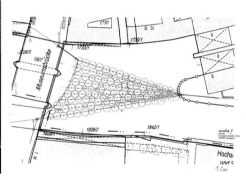

The blue balloons establish contrasts and blur boundaries: a modern installation in the heart of one of Germany's most historical cities; a blue sky floating meters above the ground, or the river rising into the air.

Audi Centenary Sculpture

Goodwood, UK

The Goodwood Festival of Speed claims to be the world's biggest and most diverse celebration of the history of motor sport and car culture. The event is held each year in Goodwood Park, whose history with motor racing dates back to the first half of the 20th century. For every event Lord March, owner of the Goodwood Estate, commissions London-based and Calcutta-born artist Gerry Judah with exuberant sculptural displays of racing cars.

For the 2009 edition Audi sponsored this enormous sculpture emplaced in front of the estate's impressive manor house, which commemorates the car giant's centenary year. The juxtaposition of the two constructions forms an aesthetical contrast: the highly classical house and the ultra-modern sculpture, highlighting Audi's long history in the industry together with the technology applied today in the company's vehicle range. The sculpture celebrates Audi's achievements in motor sport with the legendary 1937 Auto Union Streamliner and the recently launched R8 V10 sports car at either end of a dramatic "swoosh" of tire tracks, as if they are about to drive off into the sky. The piece measures an impressive 32 m (105 ft) high and weighs 44 tons.

The sculpture is made entirely of steel and although the design looks simple, it is actually the result of an extremely complex process. The structure had to be rigid and completely balanced without the need of any supporting props, with the exception of the base of the sculpture itself. In total it took 12 men four weeks to fabricate, assemble and install the structure. The piece was ideal for the festival since, besides being a marvel to look at, festival goers could even clamber about the base and have their photos taken beneath the flying cars.

Design: Gerry Judah
Client: Audi
Concept & Design: Gerry Judah
Structural Engineering: Capita Bobrowski
Steel Fabrication and Installation:
Littlehampton Welding Ltd
Photographs: David Barbour

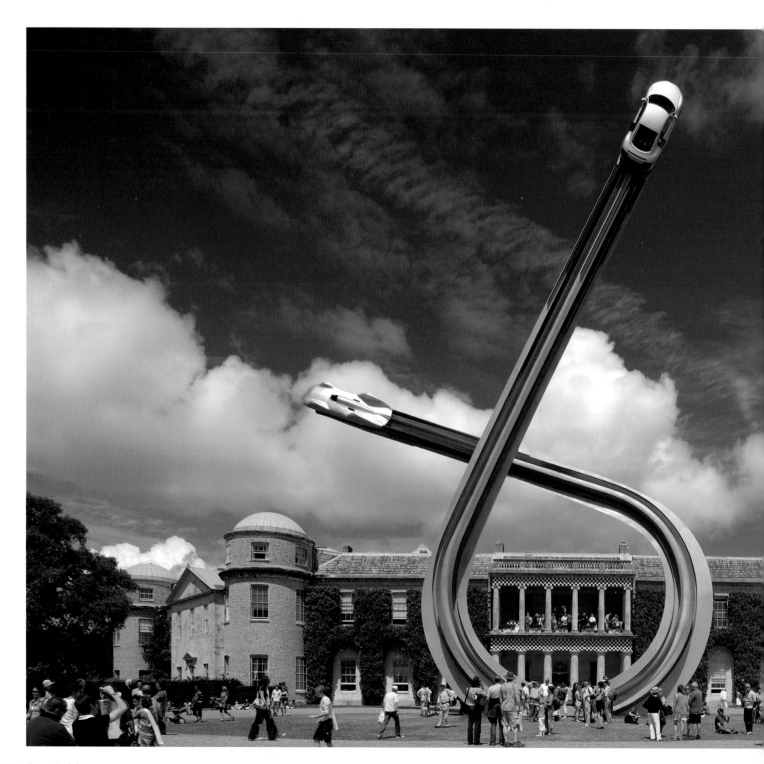

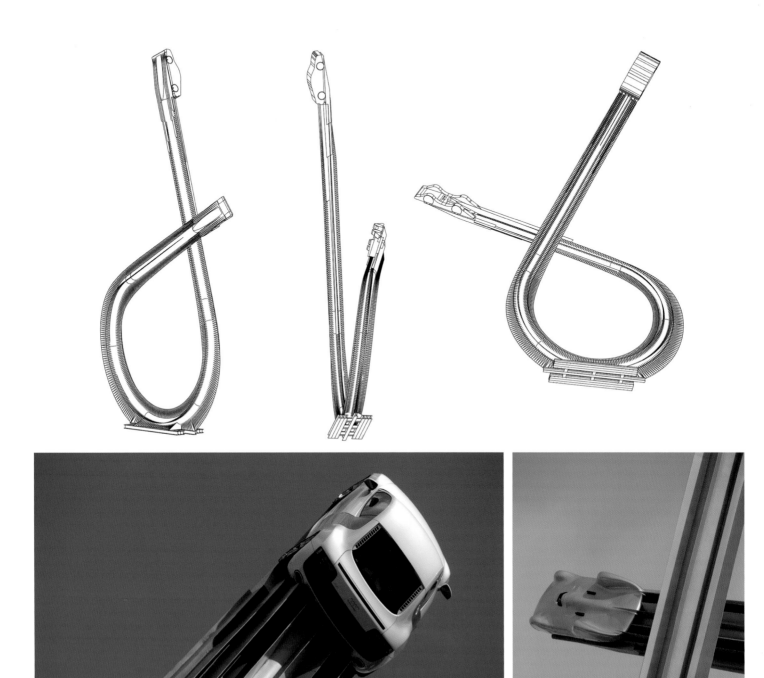

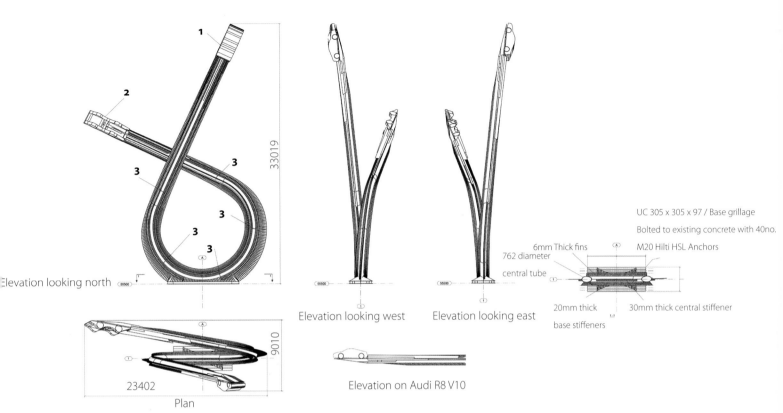

1
2
3
3
3
3
3
3

33019

Elevation looking north

9010

23402

Plan

Elevation looking west

Elevation looking east

Elevation on Audi R8 V10

UC 305 x 305 x 97 / Base grillage

Bolted to existing concrete with 40no.

M20 Hilti HSL Anchors

6mm Thick fins

762 diameter
central tube

20mm thick
base stiffeners

30mm thick central stiffener

1. Audi R8 V10
2. Auto Union streamliner
3. Site Welded joint

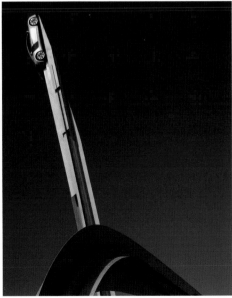

The sculpture commemorates 100 years of Audi and stands a massive 32 m (105 ft) high and was made from 44 tons of steel.